# STAY HUN

"I've witnessed Andy & Joel's trar
skills first hand. What they don . ..... .., .... . ...... ...
knowing. In this book they combine their years of
experience, testing and measuring to demonstrate the
power of their marketing system. If you're looking to
make your marketing sell, this is the book for you."

- Chris Penman, bestselling author and
director of Stark Consulting Engineers Ltd

"There are numerous marketing books out there offering
methods that are just not within reach of a business owner.
They're written for marketers themselves. Stay Hungry
is different. Andy and Joel have perfected their system
and this book to speak to those who need it most,
business decision makers looking for growth."

- Matt Harmsworth, bestselling author and
director of ROAVR Group

# STAY HUNGRY

*Andy*

*Joel*

# LEGAL NOTICES

# STAY HUNGRY

## HOW TO CREATE
## MARKETING THAT SELLS™
## EVEN IN THE NEW ECONOMY

### BE MORE VISIBLE
### REACH MORE PEOPLE
### GET MORE SALES

**ANDY RAO & JOEL STONE**

## BOOK A DISCOVERY CALL
## WITH ONE OF THE AUTHORS

Buying this book is a smart investment in your business growth. But you're still parting with your hard-earned cash and it's appreciated. So we'd like to say, "Thank you."

If you read this book and are wowed by Marketing That Sells™... but you decide you'd rather have a professional outfit implement the system for you, get in touch. The Codebreak team will action it for you at a discounted rate. Every aspect will be taken care of, from setup to management and reporting.

The beauty of outsourcing – all the results with none of the HR headaches! All you have to do is apply for a Discovery Call at: www.codebreak.co.uk/discovery-call

In Step 2 of the form, you'll see the question, 'What is your biggest frustration with your marketing / website?'

In the answer box, type in the code 'STAYHUNGRY'. And then answer the question as normal.

If your application is pre-approved, you'll be able to schedule a time for a Discovery Call. You and us, uninterrupted, talking about your business goals.

To our families,
thank you for everything

# CONTENTS

# INTRODUCTION

WELCOME to your step-by-step guide to taking your business to the next level.

Whether you're a small start-up or a long-established firm wanting to expand further, the Marketing That Sells™ system will help.

The system is tried-and-tested, you see. If you're the sort of business owner who wants the phone and the till to ring more, chances are you value strategies that have been actioned out there on the battlefield. All those internet "gurus" who've never actually owned a successful business themselves mean well but what they're often peddling is theory.

Theories don't put food on the table.

If you want to earn more money and help more people, Marketing That Sells™ is for you.

No matter where you are in your exciting business journey, start at Step 1 of Marketing That Sells™ rather than dipping in and dipping out wherever you feel.

Business growth is a process. A formula. You start with the end in mind, but you still start at the start.

You'll learn things.

You'll be reminded of things you already know.

You'll see how it all pieces together.

You'll end up with a clear plan of making more money through smarter marketing.

Let your competitors do bits of marketing in between all the firefighting. A few social media posts when they can, with no strategy driving everything. Let them spend time, effort and money without knowing the outcome. You sit back and smile, knowing what your Return On Investment is.

Marketing That Sells™ will help you increase your revenues. It will also give your day back to you. By embracing systemisation and automation, you can do more of whatever it is you love doing. Better than dealing with tyre-kickers on Facebook, sifting through statistics and trying to get your website to rank higher.

Impact. Growth. FREEDOM!

Enjoy the ride.

# STEP 1

## BY JOEL STONE

# STEP 1

# FUCK EVERYTHING ELSE UNTIL YOU'VE SORTED THIS

BY JOEL STONE

Now we have your attention…

The Marketing That Sells™ system will work for <u>any</u> business. As you read through this book, we'll take you on a step-by-step walkthrough. It's as simple as that.

However, unless you have Step 1 nailed, don't bother reading on. This system simply will not work for business owners who can't commit to Step 1.

You need to know your audience.

If there is one mistake we see most businesses make, it's trying to please too many people.

It is such an easy trap. A trap formed from one of your best intentions – helping others.

If you're the kind of businessperson who knows you have a good product or service, you know you're better than your competitors and you just can't understand why more people aren't buying, then this will resonate with you.

Not so long ago, we were working with a business owner who had a really good product on his hands. But he couldn't get it out of his head that everyone should want it.

"It doesn't matter what you think of your product or service, it's about what they think," we'd regularly explain to him.

"Who are THEY?" he'd fire back.

Exactly!

Who are they?

There are very few, if any, products or services on the planet that are meant for everyone. Every business has its niche, and there is a good reason for that.

## ED'S PLANT-BASED STORY

Now that businessperson – let's call him Ed – really couldn't grasp this. Ed was on the verge of losing it all. Not because he didn't have a good product. Not because he didn't have good business systems. The risk was that he was trying to please everybody.

Ed's meat alternative really did taste like the real thing. It even looked like the real thing. All of the ingredients were ethically sourced and even the price point was close to the real thing.

His mission, in his mind, was to replace meat. However, trying to change the behaviour of the masses overnight is no small undertaking. That kind of objective is a quick way to blow a marketing budget and lose confidence in your business.

Now, at this point, it will help if you see this from Ed's perspective...

Ed had grown up in the rural English county of Shropshire, on a small farm. Through his teen years, each day, alongside his school work, he'd help out his parents with the day-to-day tasks about the place.

It wasn't the easiest of upbringings. Unsavoury hours, manual labour no matter the weather and parents that were "working" 365 days a year.

And as each year passed, Ed saw his parents struggle more and more. The supermarkets drive a hard bargain, putting pressure on the agricultural industry, and Ed witnessed this first hand.

"There's got to be a better way!" Ed thought to himself.

At eighteen, Ed went to university to study food engineering. His now elderly parents decided to sell the farm and retire, but sadly, they divorced. Years of toil had taken their toll on their relationship.

The thought never left Ed, "There has got to be a better way!"

And that's where his business idea sprung from. A meat alternative that tastes like the real thing, can be sold for close to the same price, and better yet, you don't need loads of land and to work 365 days a year to make a living.

Ed had a huge emotional connection to his product, and rightly so. Perhaps if he'd thought of this sooner, his parents would still be together, he thought.

## AND WE'LL STOP YOU RIGHT THERE!

You have got to take yourself out of the equation. This isn't about you (or Ed).

As a business owner, this has to be about what is best for the business. Maybe you truly are the new Coca-Cola and you're set to take the world by storm – but if you try to take on the big guns too early, you'll be out of pocket before you know it.

Now is the time to be objective. How are you going to get the most marketing bang for your buck?

You need to know your audience and who they should be – and who they should be right now is the people who are most likely to buy from you.

It doesn't matter if you think everyone should buy your product or service. Who is **most** likely to buy it? Who will cost you the **least** to turn into a customer?

## YOUR CUSTOMER AVATAR

After a few months of doing it his way, the penny dropped with

Ed. He didn't have the marketing budget to convince enough lifelong meat eaters to change their behaviour and switch to his product. Maybe one day the world would change... but one step at a time.

Ed needed to figure out who was most likely to buy from him, and importantly, where to find them.

He came to the conclusion that targeting vegans and vegetarians was his best bet. And with that, he set about ensuring his product was being displayed in the vegetarian section of the shops that stocked it.

Ed was excited. He felt like he had a clear vision of who his customer should be, who his marketing should speak to and the direction his company should take.

Sales did improve, but only marginally. All that excitement drained out of Ed. He felt dejected. Perhaps his product wasn't as good as he thought.

That was when we met. It wasn't quite the last chance saloon, but it wasn't far off. Ed was at the lowest point he'd ever been with his business and he was starting to lose confidence in his product.

Now, being from rural Shropshire, it probably hadn't occurred to Ed that vegetarianism is hardly a niche anymore. In 2020, 8% of the world's population identified as vegetarian or vegan.

Our first suggestion to Ed was that people who want to eat a product that tastes and looks like meat probably liked meat in the first place. Immediately, he could narrow his audience to people that used to eat meat or are experimenting with leaving meat behind.

Ed could feel his motivation returning, like a sudden weight had been lifted off his shoulders. "I can target people on a health kick or who are looking to become vegetarian!" he exclaimed.

Ed's product was stocked in a couple of leading supermarkets and it took him 18 months to get it placed. So, there was no point in targeting people who shopped elsewhere.

The audience was starting to niche down: people interested in a meat replacement who shop in one of two places.

As we continued our discussions, we looked at the type of person that shops in those supermarkets. What gender are they? What do they drive? What brands do they like? What's their average spend? How old are they? Do they have children? The more detail we could get written down, the better.

We call this a "customer avatar". The perfect customer. The prospect that is most likely to buy from you.

For the first time, Ed felt like he had absolute clarity. He knew who his audience were, he knew where to find them and he understood for the first time why they were interested in his product.

Now why does this matter to you?

If you don't know who you're marketing to, your marketing will never work. Sorry to burst your bubble, but it needs to be done.

Not every business will be as clear and easy as Ed's. We've worked with accountants, property developers, fabric stores, business coaches, online clothing shops and many more. Every business is different.

And of course, you'll pick up customers similar to your avatar, but that's not the same as actively targeting them. Where is your marketing spend best spent?

There are some simple questions you must ask yourself to help build this picture.

## QUESTION 1
## WHO DO YOU WANT TO WORK WITH?

We don't mean what type of businesses or what sector; we mean the actual people. There is no use trying to build a business with people you resent working with or selling to. You will never achieve the freedom you desire.

Think about the sort of people you click with – those business transactions that have felt seamless.

Now, we understand that businesses grow, becoming multi-faceted and selling to all sorts of people. However, we're talking about the situation right now. What customers will make for the easiest, most cost-efficient acquisition for your business in this moment?

Think about those deals that went well. The ones that worked out great for everyone. Money was paid on time, there was mutual respect, maybe they even referred other business to you. It felt more like dealing with a friend than a customer.

Are they friendly or formal? Are they direct or nuanced? Are they considered or hurried?

There is no right or wrong type of person. It's about whatever character your business finds easiest to deal with.

That's the type of person you want to work with.

## QUESTION 2
## WHO IS YOUR PRODUCT OR SERVICE FOR?

So you've got the character sorted, but there's no point trying to sell them something they'll never buy. They might be the right personality, but you don't sell engine oil to someone who doesn't have a car.

Carefully consider who is most likely to require your product or service. Who has an immediate need?

Let's take a bottled water company. It's just launched a new eco-friendly bottled spring water. So who is this for? Everyone, right? Wrong!

There are lots of factors to niche this person down to:

- People who don't usually drink tap water
- People who are environmentally conscious
- People who opt for water ahead of soft drinks, fruit juice or sports drinks
- Younger consumers who are less likely to be prepared and carry their own water

- People in countries with restrictions on plastic bottles
- People who live in hard water areas
- People concerned about the nitrate content of tap water
- People who look for high mineral content in their water
- People who have the disposable income to pay for bottled water

So many factors for such a simple product. Looking at just these points, it's obvious you're more likely to be able to sell this water to environmentally conscious people who tend to avoid tap water, don't have time to prepare their own filtered water and look for a high mineral content in their drinks.

Who is your product or service for? When you dig a little deeper, you'll be surprised at what you come up with.

## QUESTION 3
## WHAT ARE THEIR INTERESTS?

If you're going to target the person from question one and two with your marketing, you need to know as much about them as you can. What do they do for fun? How do they exercise? What do they watch on TV? What do they read? In this part, you can really go to town with the detail.

We'll take the same example as before. Someone who is environmentally conscious, avoids tap water, doesn't have time to prepare filtered water and opts for high mineral content in their drinks.

Chances are they are well read, they understand the environmental impact of their choices and they know about the importance of vitamins and minerals. They lead a busy life, so they're probably not yet retired. They're not a planner or a prepper.

Let's look at what their interests could be:

- Fun and leisure: gym, after work drinks

- TV shows: Attenborough documentaries, late night TV
- Reads: non-fiction, lifestyle guides, health books

See? You really can start to build a picture.

At this point, many business owners start to think about all the other people they might be able to sell to. But that would be missing the point. This is less about who you might be able to sell to and all about who you should be trying to sell to.

Who is most likely to buy off you or easiest for your business to sell to? This is where your marketing investment should go.

## QUESTION 4 – WHAT ARE THEIR PERSONAL CIRCUMSTANCES?

Without knowing the situation someone lives in, how can you possibly know how to communicate with them?

Where do they live? Are they married? Do they have children?

This really matters. Single people make different buying decisions to married people. People with children have different priorities again. And they all might as well speak a different language. A man with two children lives in a completely different world to a single woman living in a city apartment.

Let's go back to the bottled water example. We've outlined a person with a busy life, potentially quite young, who has no time to prepare and who is both environmentally and health conscious.

It sounds like they're old enough not to be living care-free. They have responsibilities, hence why they're busy and concerned about their health and the environment. A safe bet is they're in their twenties, co-habiting but probably not married and they're yet to have children.

## QUESTION 5
## WHAT BRANDS DO THEY ENGAGE WITH?

Blimey, this is getting deep, isn't it? Bear with us. This is the last question. And it'll soon become apparent why it's so important. What cars do they like? What clothing brands do they wear? What food brands do they buy?

What you may not realise is that nowadays, advertising is smart. You can actively target people based on their interests, behaviours and the demographic they belong to. The more information you have on your perfect customer, the better.

Again, using our previous example...

• Cars: hybrid engine vehicles and electric vehicles because they're environmentally conscious (think Tesla, Toyota, Lexus, etc.)
• Clothing: eco-friendly brands like People Tree and Moral Fibres
• Food: health food products and clean eating like Pukka, Gosh and Huel

We're getting a clearer picture of this person now, so let's put it all together.

• Age: 20s
• Living situation: cohabiting
• Children: none
• Attitude: health conscious, environmentally aware, busy professional
• Fun and leisure: gym, after work drinks
• TV: Attenborough documentaries, late night TV
• Reading: non-fiction, lifestyle guides, health books
• Brands: Tesla, Toyota, Lexus, People Tree, Moral Fibres, Pukka, Gosh, Huel

Everyone drinks water, right? Well, yes. But not everyone drinks your water. So don't waste your marketing investment on people who might, when there are plenty of people who will.

Before you move on through this guide, ask yourself who your customer avatar is. Use these five simple questions to get you going:

Question 1 – Who do you want to work with?
Question 2 – Who is your product or service for?
Question 3 – What are their interests?
Question 4 – What are their personal circumstances?
Question 5 – What brands do they engage with?

The steps in this book will show you what you need to put in place to take advantage of the Marketing That Sells™ system – the system Ed used to take his business from one that lost money to a business that gave him and his family a "better way".

# STEP 2

## BY ANDY RAO

# STEP 2

# AGREE YOUR BRAND AND TONE

## BY ANDY RAO

OK, so you've got your audience nailed. As the bishop said to the actress.

You know that by trying to appeal to everyone, you'll appeal to no one.

You can see your ideal customer in front of you. In everything you do, he or she is who you're designing for and writing for. Veer to the left or to the right a little bit, but always come back home. It's like a good book – the story may go off on a tangent here and there, but it will always bring you back to its central spine.

So, it doesn't matter what you like. It doesn't matter what your best friend likes. It doesn't matter what anyone likes unless they're your ideal customer. Someone who will put their hand in their pocket.

You friends may love you, but even if they fit the right demographic, they probably won't want to pay or pay full price for whatever it is you're selling.

Please, please remember that everyone is an expert on someone else's business. BECAUSE IT'S NOT THEIR MONEY! They're an expert with someone else's kids and pets too. You know the kind. The person who gives you parenting advice whilst their own kids are running around trashing your house... the little shits.

Be confident in you and your learning. Only listen to successful businesspeople. Those who dish out unsolicited advice freely may not be qualified to do so. They'll be time vampires too, guaranteed. Once you've listened patiently that first time, they'll be in your ear all the time.

Protect your time ruthlessly.

## YOUR BRAND BIBLE

Anyway, where were we? Right, thinking about your ideal customer.

You know who they are, what they do, what they like and how they speak. The content you put out there – from a social media post to a press ad or a video – needs to appeal to them in how it looks and how it reads. Every time.

If you create a piece of marketing and something in it jars with them, that's a potential sale lost. People like consistency and they don't even know it. Because then comes familiarity, then trust and then a sale.

No messing about here. You'll benefit from creating a Brand Bible, which everyone in your business must read and read again. Whether they work in marketing or accounts.

McDonald's is a great example of a consistent brand and tone. Have a look at their Instagram, Facebook, website... whatever, it doesn't matter. They'll look the same and sound the same, reinforcing who they are. If you like them, you'll carry on liking them. If you don't like them, you'll go away. Either way, job done. They're not trying to appeal to everyone. They focus on the people who already love them or who are most likely to become lovers.

## BRAND VALUES

What do you stand for? Does your team know? If they don't,

you'd definitely benefit from listing your brand values in your Brand Bible, as this is what should be driving you all towards a common goal.

Come up with i) a strapline, ii) mission statement and iii) brand values. Codebreak's are:

- Marketing That Sells™
- Help people and have fun
- ✓ Stay hungry
- ✓ Start with 'why'
- ✓ Impress with results
- ✓ Read and lead
- ✓ Systemise and automate
- ✓ Be confident but humble
- ✓ Get out of your comfort zone
- ✓ Own your shit

Our values are framed on our wall, so we are reminded of them every day. They're what makes us, us!

To be honest, it's great marketing for clients and potential clients too. Put them on your website. Post about them on social media. It's you standing for stuff, which is a quick way to build a tribe. If someone were to ask one of your customers what your business is all about, and they don't really know what to say apart from telling them what you sell, then you'd be in a weaker position than you need to be.

If someone in your team doesn't align with these values, well, they ain't for you. If a client doesn't respect these values, then they ain't for you either.

A great read on brand values is Delivering Happiness by the late Tony Hsieh.

For a book that's meant to be focussing on results, this all may sound a bit "woo-woo". But if you're not all rowing as one, your ship won't reach its destination. Well, it might, but it will cost you in time, energy, focus and sleep. Your sanity, basically.

"Your brand is what other people say about you when you're not in the room." - Jeff Bezos, Founder of Amazon

## DESIGN

The first thing people will see in your marketing is your branding. Predominantly, how your website looks and how your social media posts look.

So, what colours and fonts and font sizes should you be using to appeal to your customer avatar?

No point using tiny font sizes if your average customer is 70. So many businesses don't even consider this. It doesn't matter if you have the prettiest website in the world – if people struggle to read it, especially on a mobile, they'll be outta there faster than Usain Bolt on speed.

Thinking about the colours you use is a good start. Do you have a primary colour, secondary colour and then perhaps one or two tertiary colours? We know so many businesses that use whatever colours they fancy in their social media imagery. It almost depends on what mood they're in that day!

Nay, nay and thrice nay.

You won't see a McDonald's franchisee playing about with the shade of yellow in the golden arches, or deciding to add purple to their menus. Even if you don't know McDonald's colours off by heart, when you see them, you know it's them.

We had a new refrigeration company come to us to create their brand. Guess what the business owner's favourite colour was?

Yup, red.

Red and the cold do not go hand in hand. It just wouldn't compute with people. You'd need to go down the blue route, otherwise you'd be ice skating uphill from the off. This doesn't mean you have to look like every other refrigeration company in the world

– far from it – but don't be different for different's sake. It's a balancing act.

A simple Google search will show you what colours are associated with what feelings they emote. Trust, strength and so on. If this is something you've never considered, go do some Googling now. Even lay down the law on images. *These are the kinds of images we use in our business. Always colour, never black and white. Always people, never without people.* Whatever you decide. But by showing a spread of approved imagery in your Brand Bible, you'll be giving your employees a good handle on what fits your brand.

Maybe you'll take it a step further and source or take lots of photos yourself. *No other photos except these.* You can add to the gallery when you want and remove images when you want. When they've been used a few times already, say. This is why storing images in a shared folder, like Dropbox, is best. It means you're all working from the same resource. You remove a picture and it's removed for everyone.

When it comes to your social media image templates, design them in a tool like Canva. Your employees will have no excuse. *Here are two templates for quotes. Here are three templates for special offers. Do not deviate from these.* If your guys can't follow these instructions, someone else needs to take over your marketing.

It may seem like you're trying to stifle creativity, but believe me, simple processes work. You can't let staff go off half-cocked.

Let's come back to Maccie D's. Why do you think they're so successful? Because decades ago, Ray Kroc systemised everything. *Here's how to do a burger. Here's how to do fries. Here's how many gherkin slices to use. Do that, you'll do well. Deviate, you're sacked.*

If someone does have an idea to improve your templates, by all means, bring it to the table and then you decide. Don't let them run off with it without consulting you.

We've seen many an employee bring a business almost to its knees because they've been left to do whatever they want. Their intentions are admirable, but it's only the results that count.

## LANGUAGE

Based on your customer avatar, decide on the kind of language you use. Formal? Fun? Quirky? A bit sweary? Whatever you decide, you stick with it. Your team doesn't deviate from it. If you don't have an employed team but outsource your marketing and design, they need to have your Bible.

If you're going down the formal language route, be careful. Even traditionally "stiff" sectors such as accountancy and HR don't have to be. In fact, if you're in a stuffy industry, this could be your opportunity to shake it up a bit and disrupt. With the onslaught of tech and social media, times and tones are changing. If all your competitors wear suits, wear jeans. If all your competitors wear jeans, wear a suit.

At Codebreak, we wear our branded "Stay Hungry" t-shirts and hoodies. It's good advertising for us. Plus, it reinforces that we're a crew when we turn up for meetings and expos. But most importantly, everyone else in our industry wears shirts and sports jackets. Usually with shit-flicker shoes.

Be different, *if* you can handle it.

In your Brand Bible, write down a load of phrases and words that reflect who you are. Like a dictionary and thesaurus rolled into one. Also write down phrases and words that must not be used. Upon pain of death.

What phrases do all your competitors use? Add them to the naughty list straightaway.

Your language will help set you apart from the off.

> *Adjective, n. a word naming an attribute of a noun*
> *Adverb, n. a word or phrase that modifies or qualifies an adjective or verb*

We're not massive fans of the overuse of adjectives and adverbs, although they have become commonplace. So, to be honest, we're looking at this as another opportunity! We don't like weak, lazy words such as "very" either.

Something isn't "very good"; it's "awesome".

Something isn't "very bad"; it's "awful".

"Really", "so" and "such" are similar.

Here's why we're not fans of flowery language.

Subconsciously, it tells the reader that what you're offering isn't good enough on its own. It needs embellishing. The new car you're selling doesn't just go fast; it goes "super-fast". The new beer you're selling doesn't just taste wonderful; it tastes "unbelievably wonderful".

Use adjectives and adverbs, by all means, but don't fall into the trap of using them all the time. It will weaken your message.

The only time lots of adjectives and adverbs *may* work is if you're targeting younger people and women. (Don't shoot the messenger.)

If you're worried that your marketing language is overly flowery, go buy *Ogilvy on Advertising*. It's outdated in terms of certain attitudes, but you won't find better advice on copywriting that sells.

As you can tell, we love templates and systemisation. It's because it works for the big boys. By applying big company thinking to small businesses, you'll enjoy the best of both worlds. Also, most employees appreciate order. They may fancy themselves as the new Elon Musk or *enfant terrible* of entrepreneurship, but deep down, they take comfort in clear structure.

## HOW DO YOU MAKE ME FEEL?

Maya Angelou said: "People will forget what you said, people will forget what you did, but people will never forget how you made them feel."

Your design and language need to come together to position your business as you want it to be positioned.

If you want to convey serious luxury, you don't want to be using Comic Sans font anywhere.

If you want to convey cheap and cheerful, you don't want to be handing out business cards with velvet lamination and gold foil lettering.

I'll never forget a financial adviser coming to a breakfast meeting and banging on about how he was only interested in high-net-worth individuals. He gave me his card and it was the cheapest card I'd ever seen. He'd even crossed out the phone number and written his new number in biro. And I was supposed to trust him with my mum's life savings? Hmm…

Whether we like it or not, perception is reality.

If you sell a premium product or service, you can't look cheap. If necessary, fake it until you make it. Make sacrifices in other areas. Don't tell me you can't fork out £100 for decent business cards when you're smoking 20 cigarettes a day. That's the price of doing business.

The main feeling to focus on is trust. Every business will benefit from eliciting trust in their customers and potential customers.

New customers – trust alleviates buyer's remorse, that itch you get when you've just bought something and wonder whether you've made the right decision.

Established customers – trust makes it more likely they will buy off you again and recommend you.

Prospects – trust keeps them interested in you.

So be humble, yet confident in everything you say. People won't trust someone who's unsure about what they're saying. Whether you're unsure of the "script" or your actual product or service, uncertainty ain't good! It's like starting off a prospecting email apologising for taking up their time. NO! Never apologise unless you've done something wrong.

Be OK with having an opinion and sharing it publicly, even if you think others may disagree. Unless you're actually saying something unethical, of course – then you should shut up! Definitely stay away from race, politics and religion. But when you shrink away from voicing your thoughts, you lose the opportunity to resonate with someone.

To avoid criticism… say nothing, do nothing, be nothing. Aristotle said that thousands of years ago, so we've got no excuse.

You see, fear can be the ruin of many a small business. Fear of getting out of your comfort zone. Even voicing an opinion can be scary. This is why it's important you read up on mindset, <u>always</u>. There's no point having the best marketing strategy in the world if you haven't got the cojones to implement it.

Clearing up your brand and tone will build you a tribe. Be famous to a few. Forget trying to become everyone's friend.

## PREQUALIFYING PEOPLE WILL SAVE YOU TIME AND MORE

If you're selling a high volume of widgets online, the type of person buying off you perhaps isn't as important. But even then, I assume you'd like them to come back, buy more and recommend you. Correct?

If you're selling a lower volume of high-end products, like cars for example, and certainly if you're selling a service, your marketing design and language will attract the right people and put off the wrong people. I can't stress that enough. You have to be OK with that. Don't worry about the people who prefer Pepsi when you're selling Coca-Cola. Look after your Coca-Cola fans and go after people who like Fanta, and so on.

All the time, energy, focus and money it takes to try and convert the wrong type of person is, well… it's not worth it. Plus, even if they do convert and sign on the dotted line, chances are they'll be a royal pain in the arse.

So, if your marketing conveys a luxury feel, don't worry about Bob who figures he wouldn't be able to afford you then goes around telling all his friends that you're expensive. Bob's friends will be like him, so this will save you a whole bunch of time! You want to disqualify Bob and his mates as quickly and as easily as possible. Your brand and tone will do this – if you get it right. It's such an important foundation, even though it may reside in the "super boring" file.

And remember to think exactly like that about pricing. It's not that you're too expensive; they just can't afford you. That's the reality, and that's *their* problem. People will always shift blame and/or responsibility onto someone else.

Let me tell you what will cost you more – having to rebrand in the future because you got it wrong the first time around.

## WHAT IF I'VE REALISED I NEED TO DO SOMETHING ABOUT MY BRAND?

Don't worry, you may not have to rebrand.

If you're now suspecting that your website, social media and marketing collateral might not be up to scratch, bringing in "little" changes over time will probably do the trick. Nailing down social media templates, changing a few images around on your website, working new phrasing into your ads...

The important thing is you're taking action. You've decided to have a Brand Bible and clarify what you're all about. Who you are, who you help, how and why. Everyone in your team follows this until it becomes second nature. Include checklists if necessary. There's nothing wrong with that. When we're called in to troubleshoot for a marketing team, you wouldn't believe how many times someone has said to us, "I don't need a checklist to do that task..." and then they cock something up. Checklists are good.

If your colours aren't the most appropriate for your industry or vision, you might need to bite the bullet and re-brand.

Perhaps you're a solicitor, your main colour is green and you're now thinking you look like a recycling firm... You may have to rip that plaster off. You can get away with changing words and phraseology, but changing your primary colour from green to blue overnight is a biggie, which is why you may need to re-brand.

Look at it as an opportunity for free PR! It will need to happen at some point. Do it now, then you won't have to do it later, as an old boss of mine used to say. Wise words that have served Codebreak well. It's too easy to put things off these days.

If you decide to re-brand, tell your customers first. Assure them that nothing is changing in your service or pricing; this is simply the next step in your growth. People like to deal with businesses that are growing, but that still retain the personal touch. Tell them your company name, number and bank details are staying the same too, so they don't think you're phoenixing.

Ultimately, remember that no one will care about your baby as much as you. You may worry what people will think about your re-brand... but guess what? They've got their own shit to deal with.

# STEP 3

## BY JOEL STONE

# STEP 3

# PREPARE YOUR WEBSITE TO HELP YOU SELL

## BY JOEL STONE

With Marketing That Sells™, we always look at the final point of sale, or when an enquiry is made. If your website enquiry form doesn't work or your e-commerce shop is too complicated, then we're sorry to tell you that you've got bigger problems than your marketing.

If your website ain't right, sort it NOW!

Traditionally, the job of marketing is to collect leads. It's the job of your website/sales person/vending machine to turn that lead into a sale. Marketing That Sells™ would be a crap name for a system if it didn't include selling.

You will have a good idea about the websites in your industry. The better ones are probably quite polished, feature good photography and perhaps list the benefits of what the business offers. You could jump from any industry to another and most websites will all follow that same format. *Here is who we are, this is what we do, and these are the benefits.*

## THESE WEBSITES DO NOT HELP THOSE BUSINESSES SELL.

Now that might come as a shock to you. Bet you've seen some beautiful websites. In the marketing industry, there are literally thousands of examples of this kind of website.

The thing is, these companies aren't thinking about it from the customer's perspective. The prospect wants to know what's in it for them. So what do you provide that none of your competitors can get near? It could be the problem you solve, the money you save your customers, the guarantee you offer. But how does it impact the person looking at your website?

## MAGICAL ME*

*For you Harry Potter fans out there

Stop talking about yourself. Honestly, nobody cares.

Ironic statement for two guys writing a book about their own marketing system, but hear us out.

Very few people will buy from you because they care about you. They buy from you because of how it will help them. Take you, the reader of this book. Chances are you're reading this book to improve your marketing know-how. You're not reading it so that we can tell you a list of the plus points of our system.

So how does this book help you, the reader? Well, if you read the cover, you'll know it's going to help you create Marketing That Sells™, even in the new economy, so that you're more visible, able to reach more people and make more sales. This is about you.

Let's walk through an example...

We recently worked with a luxury chocolatier. Artisan chocolates at artisan prices! We're not talking about your average chocolate bar here.

To give you an idea, a box of six chocolate truffles cost £22 and a large box of 24 chocolates cost £70. Chocolate for true chocolate lovers. People who know their onions (or chocolate).

Sheila (she wasn't called Sheila), the owner, had been fortunate enough to negotiate a large space at Harrods in the early days of her business and many of her orders came directly from there or through repeat telephone orders from choccy connoisseurs. However, with more and more competitors joining the market online, she was starting to feel the squeeze.

That's when she spoke to us. She'd been selling through an online shop for a couple of years. She always considered it bonus income. Orders without the effort. That was, in her words, her "pocket money".

We had a quick look over her website. Her traffic was incredible. A serious number of visitors to her website every day. This should have meant more than just "pocket money", but the sales weren't there to back up the website visits.

## AUDIT YOUR WEBSITE...
## OR GET IT AUDITED

We sent Sheila a report of our findings...

A homepage that showcases the artisan process, an about page that talks about the history of the brand, a contact page with a cut-and-paste enquiry form and tucked away was a shop, with one image per product, product titles (but no descriptions), no reviews and no clear method of payment.

It was a bloody miracle that she'd made any online sales at all!

If somebody read the brand history, there was no clear journey to a sale. If somebody checked out the artisan process, again, they hit a dead end.

We talked to Sheila about making her product the centrepiece of her website and how reviews would provide social proof. Sheila even had testimonials from some of the world's leading chocolatiers, but these were nowhere to be seen.

Everything needed addressing.

How could the digital experience offered by her website be similar to the experience her customers get in Harrods?

In Harrods, the salesperson doesn't stand there and tell you the entire store history whilst simultaneously reeling off a list of all the benefits of their organisation. They draw you in with a smile, they offer you a sample, they tell you the story of where the cocoa was carefully sourced and that no one chocolate is exactly the same as another. You're salivating before they've even finished talking.

That experience needed to be recreated on the website. A video of a renowned chocolate taster, customer reviews, the story of how that truffle came to be and how much love went into making it. By the time the user has realised they're entering their card details, they should feel like they're in a boutique version of Willy Wonka's Chocolate Factory.

A luxury product should take the user away from the ordinary, away from the mundane. It should give them a sense of something better. People don't buy £70 chocolate because it tastes nice. A Kit-Kat tastes nice! They buy luxury chocolate to be part of something. For escapism. They'll buy it purely to show off that they can. Sheila needed to guide them to that decision.

So we worked with Sheila to rearrange the website, which eventually became her greatest source of revenue. Maybe she refers to Harrods as "pocket money" now. We doubt it.

What does this mean for your website?

## CATEGORY OF <u>ONE</u>

Your website is more than just a brochure of your services. 99% of the people who intend to buy from you will check out your website at some point. Now, if it's beautiful and looks professional, you probably won't put them off. But what about all the visitors who are just shopping around, doing some research, or thinking about it?

If you're anything like us, when you need a new vacuum cleaner, you don't just buy the first one you come across. You research the best suck for your buck. (You'll never forget that line.)

James Dyson recognised this, and he did something incredibly smart to outwit his competitors. He put his vacuum cleaner in a category of one.

"New cyclone technology," said the ads when Dyson launched. What he offered wasn't comparable to his competitors because it was distinctly different. Ultimately, it achieved the same thing. But who knew? With "new cyclone technology", maybe your carpet would be that much cleaner! It sure sounds like it should be!

The next time you're looking at one of your products or services on your website, picture swapping your logo for your leading competitor's logo. Does it make any difference? Could all of the benefits you've listed be applied to any old business in your industry?

Remember, stop talking about yourself, nobody cares. And even worse if you could be talking about any business in your industry.

Take a step back. How does your product or service positively impact the lives of your potential customers? That is what your website should be about.

There are four key elements to your website that should be addressed before launching your next marketing campaign:

1. Functionality
2. Language
3. Brand
4. Journey

## FUNCTIONALITY

Firstly, if you're one of those businesses that isn't sure if your website works properly on a mobile phone, find out right now. We've got clients with 90% of their traffic coming from mobile. If the user experience on mobile is awful, you're missing a trick. A big trick.

When we say "functionality", we basically mean "does your website work?".

There's no use having a website that sends people to a 404 error page when people try and navigate. Or a website where the contact forms don't work. You might be thinking, "Well, duh", but you'd be surprised. There are some big companies out there with contact forms that you fill in, think you've contacted them, and yet that form has gone nowhere. Make sure yours work.

Five things to check about website functionality:

1. Loading speed: does your website load and function in an acceptable time?
2. Links: do they all work?
3. Forms: do they all work?
4. Navigation: can a user navigate around the website?
5. Platform: does the website work equally well on a mobile, tablet, laptop and desktop?

If you plan for your marketing to drive people to your website, get your website functionality in check. We've seen some incredible marketing campaigns that drive loads of traffic and achieve a grand total of bugger all because they fall down at the final hurdle – the website.

## LANGUAGE

What language does your potential customer talk?

We don't mean English or French. We mean how they talk. What sort of words do they use? When they're thinking about your product or service, what buzzwords spring to their mind?

Urgh. Buzzwords. That's a disgusting term. Every industry has them. Ignore the industry terms. We don't mean those. In marketing we have "key performance indicators" and "search engine optimisation". Two of the fastest terms to turn a customer off.

Get those industry buzzwords out of your head now. Reset.

Now imagine your customer is in the pub chatting to their mates. How would they describe your product then?

Let's look at an example. This time we've taken some wording from a tyre company's consumer website (not a website for tyre geeks).

They've described their tyres like this:

* Premium surface anchoring
* Asymmetrical tread pattern
* Optimised notches

What they actually mean is this:

* Great road grip
* The pattern isn't symmetric, so the tyres perform equally well in the wet and dry
* There are little grooves in the tyres to aid braking

But that doesn't sound all that special, does it? So what does the customer really want to hear?

Think back to Dyson and his "new cyclone technology". He knew people might not be able to comprehend that, so he demonstrated it with little whirlwinds in the TV adverts. Remember those? He made the connection for the customer.

So, what should the tyre company do to speak to the consumer? Remember, they're not a tyre geek...

* Market-leading road grip
* Fantastic performance in all conditions
* Reduced braking distance

Now the language is appropriate to the potential customer and still explains the benefits specific to those tyres. If you can't speak to your potential customer in their lingo, they won't know you're able to solve their problem.

You've got to be relatable. It isn't professional to be able to spout all of your industry terms and baffle people. That's the opposite of professional. Smart people can explain the most complex things in simple terms.

It's actually easy to make this mistake, especially if you work in your industry every day. Some of your day-to-day terminology is second nature to you. It might feel unbelievable to you that people don't know what you're talking about.

"Remarketing" is a term we often use. Everyone in our team knows exactly what it means. We say it all the time. We've dedicated a whole step to it in the Marketing That Sells™ process. It would be easy for us to expect you to know what it means, but why would you? We'll explain later.

Think about the buzzwords (urgh) your consumers use around your product or service, not the terminology you're used to using. What language excites them? What language explains things to them? What language makes you sound amazing, without over-complicating matters?

## BRAND

Many small businesses have websites that look nothing like the rest of their brand. But remember, today's consumer is smarter than that. Most people support a sports team, or like a fashion brand, or have a favourite fast-food restaurant. They're used to and expect consistent branding.

If your website doesn't match up with the rest of your brand, it won't make sense to the user. You're immediately planting a seed of doubt…

"Hang on, is this the same company? Why is their website different?"

Imagine you've got your marketing campaign firing on all cylinders. Great news! But then the potential customer fails to purchase because you thought it was a good idea to mess with the colours on your website. *Sigh…* Just don't do it.

Brand consistency has multiple benefits that help with selling. To ignore them is to put your business at a disadvantage.

If your logo, colours, key messages and style flow through all your materials, then you are consistently moulding the perception of your brand. If that suddenly changes, all that hard work is undone.

If your marketing campaign·has worked, chances are you've tied a positive emotional reaction to your brand. When a customer visits your website and everything matches up, that emotion will be recalled.

But brand consistency isn't just about the visuals; it's about the language and the user experience. If your campaign has taken the user on a journey, using certain language in a certain way and then that suddenly feels different, you risk halting their progress.

Think about the major brands in the world. It doesn't matter if you visit the Chinese version of their website or the American version – it will look and feel the same. This builds trust and loyalty. People know what they're getting. They feel comfortable. They feel safe.

And to top it all off, if you want to differentiate your business from your competitors, you best get that brand consistency nailed down. We've mentioned the mistake of everyone looking the same. Leverage your brand to keep in touch with your audience. Become familiar to them. Alienate your competitors.

## JOURNEY

Everyone is on a journey now, aren't they? A health journey, a mindset journey, a journey of bloody discovery.

"Customer journey" is another wanky phrase us marketing types like to use, but it is important. It's an easy way to describe the steps you expect your website users to take. The first website page they'll land on and where they'll go from there. Literally, the journey they will go on through your website.

## THIS SHOULD NOT BE GUESSWORK.

What do you want the user to do? Make it abundantly clear. Spell it out to them.

If you sell a product and it isn't easy to add that product to the basket within a couple of clicks, your website is wrong. If you sell a service and at any point on the website you can't see a clear way to enquire about that service, your website is wrong.

Brutal. But Marketing That Sells™ sometimes needs to be brutal about home truths. If you want results, you need to strip out any issues before they arise. You will know from a quick look at your website if it's letting you down on this point.

Not all websites are about the immediate sell, or an enquiry. They might form part of your campaign, they might act as a community, they might be informative. The same rule still applies. If it isn't abundantly clear what the user needs to do, you'll be missing out on whatever engagement it is you require from them.

Think of it like a corner shop. Following the rise of the supermarkets, the smart corner shop owners realised that most people only came into their store for essentials. Milk, bread – that sort of thing.

The *really* smart owners placed these items at the back of the store. Then the customer had to walk past all the special offers and all the premium items before they could grab their essentials and make their return journey to the till. Chances are they bought more than they initially intended to.

This is the same principle. What do you need your users to do before they leave your website? What do they need to see? What do they need to read? What do they need to do?

If you've run a marketing campaign before and had loads of traffic to your website but no enquiries or sales, chances are one of these four key elements was wrong. It didn't function like it should, you didn't speak their language, it didn't look trustworthy, or you took the user on the wrong journey.

Make sure your website is ready to sell.

# STEP 4

## BY ANDY RAO

# STEP 4

## BUILD YOUR SOCIAL FOUNDATIONS

BY ANDY RAO

Social media isn't going away.

When we started out in business in the mid-2000s, about 1/3 of the business owners we spoke to thought that the internet was a fad. All they needed was *The Yellow Pages* and word of mouth.

It's still the same with social media. Maybe not for 1/3 of business owners, but still a fair few. And there are definitely those out there who are only using social media because it's free. They haven't stopped for one minute to wonder what results they can actually expect to achieve from a free service.

But you're a smart business owner. You've already invested in this book. So let's assume you know social media will play an integral part in your success (and that you need to pay for social media ads). Because social media, when used properly, can do AMAZING things for your business. Any business.

Social media is used by people of all ages with all manner of interests. Thinking you can't reach enough meaningful people through social media is burying your head in the sand. Any Google search will tell you that.

Social media enables you to put your problem-solving genius in front of lots of people. If your content is interesting, you'll get in front of them time and time again. And we all know the worst number in marketing is one. If your content is *uninteresting*, you'll slip further and further down in people's timelines. More on organic social media content in a bit.

I do stress the "doing it properly" part. Leave the amateurs to run their "like and share" competitions on Facebook. Let the salespeople post 20 times a day. We're interested in getting <u>results</u> from your social.

What would you rather have from a post – 50 likes or 5 sales?

## WHICH SOCIAL MEDIA?

We get asked this a lot. If you're a big business and have a big marketing team, fill your boots. Be everywhere.

If you're a humble SME, don't spread yourself too thin. Do your research and choose two or three social media channels that will move you closer to your goals. Better to do two or three well than all of them so-so. There are only so many hours in the day and we want you to be achieving better results by working smarter. (Fancy talk for working less.)

As a broad rule of thumb, if you're Business to Business, go with Facebook and LinkedIn.

Business to Consumer, Facebook and Instagram.

If you're an author, journo or celeb, you'll probably want Twitter in the mix. According to coschedule.com, the optimal posting frequency for Twitter success is 15 times a day. Most business owners simply haven't got that amount of time. Or, if they have, that's probably why they're not successful.

Facebook, at the time of writing, is the big winner IF you utilise Facebook Advertising. (More on Facebook Ads later – a lot more.) Don't bother using Facebook if you can't or won't pay for ads. Trying to get momentum on Facebook without paying for ads should be the next *Mission Impossible* film. A few less stunts but just as hard. Again, you're smart – you know this already.

To be clear – it doesn't matter whether your target audience is on Facebook or not. Facebook's advertising platform partners with a tonne of external websites. Remember, when you see an ad on a website, chances are it's hosted by Facebook or Google. Mark Zuckerberg didn't get to where he is by being stupid.

If you'd like the ins and outs of making money through Facebook, we've put together a 13,000-word PDF you can download by visiting:

www.codebreak.co.uk/facebook-pdf-offer

## LOVE A BIO

People love reading social media bios. So if you're using a social media channel for business, make sure you've filled out the bio. Upload a decent profile photo or logo, a decent cover pic and write why your business is the best thing since sliced bread. Depending on how much room you've got, you want to convey what you do, who for, how and why.

If you've got a strapline, use it in your bio prominently, maybe even your mission statement too. If you haven't got a strapline, come up with one. As discussed in Step 2, it should be a part of your Brand Bible.

The important thing is to fill out your bio as much as you're allowed to. Share as much salient info about your business as you can, again, remembering the <u>why</u>. Telling people *what* you do will not sell you.

"We've been established since 1988…" No one cares.

"We have 20 offices across the UK…" So what?

It's something that most social media bios and websites do. Don't be like everyone else. Think benefits. Think pain-solving.

One of the most important things about marketing that hardly anybody realises is that **people would rather avoid pain than seek pleasure**. Take that nugget to your grave.

People would rather avoid pain than seek pleasure.

This will dictate so much of your sales and marketing copy.

**N.B.** Fill out all the simple stuff in your social media bios too.

It's amazing how many times we've seen the phone number or email address missing! Make it easy for people to contact you.

## WHAT TO POST

Variety is the spice of life, and your socials should be the same. If you're a lawyer and all you bang on about is your legal practice, social media won't work for you. If you're a beauty therapist and all you bang on about is your beauty salon... well, you catch my drift.

Don't go all left field and never talk about your business, of course. But you should also share insights into your industry, into complementary industries, the people you help, stories about what motivates you, as well as things that people are generally interested in that may have nothing to do with your job. Sport, music, film, the weather... whatever.

Mix it up a bit. You know your audience. What are they most interested in, besides themselves?

In addition to mixing up the content, mix up the format. Use photos, videos, quote cards, links to your website, links to other people's websites. You can also share other people's content. Who are the movers and shakers in your industry? Follow them, and if one day you're not feeling inspirational, share something inspirational from their accounts. Easy peasy.

Keep all your own content on-brand, naturally, as per Step 2. It's tempting to mess about with fonts on quote cards and so on... but don't.

When we say "quote cards", this commonly means an excerpt from an article that you've written. Like a soundbite. Or it could be a quote from somebody famous. Nothing too cheesy though, please. Lots of people go "twee" all the time and, unless your audience is twee, forget it.

The best kind of quote card will be a testimonial, taking customers' Google Reviews and Facebook Recommendations and branding them up.

With any kind of quote card, the text needs to be legible on a mobile phone. Not in text so small you'd need a telescope to see it. So if you're planning on using a long quote and shrinking the font size is the only way to fit it all in, stop. Rip out the best one or two lines and go with that.

Photos and videos are awesome. Self-generated, ideally, rather than any kind of stock. Someone in your business needs to get in front of the camera. You haven't got a choice these days. But you'll do what it takes, right? Contrary to popular opinion, a truckload of fancy tech is not required. A decent smartphone can take care of most of your social media photo and video needs.

## REUSE AND REPURPOSE

Just because you've posted something once, doesn't mean that it can never be used again. Most people won't have seen it the first time around. Or the second time around. Don't post the same things day after day, but re-use, for sure. If you post something cool on Facebook on Monday, post it on LinkedIn on Tuesday, and then maybe again in two weeks' time. Tweak the text slightly and perhaps even get it scheduled a third time.

Do schedule your social media posts if you can. There is a raft of social media scheduling tools. You're no doubt familiar with names such as Hootsuite and Buffer. Facebook is possessive and wants you to use its own scheduling facility for Facebook and Instagram. Some say they'll reduce your reach if you use a third party.

Just be careful that your posts don't become too robotic when you schedule in big chunks. Sitting there for hours on end writing post after post… well, you may lose some of your creative spark. Sometimes posting on the fly can work the best. You make the call on what works best for you.

As well as reusing, you can repurpose certain kinds of content. Video is the best example.

Shoot a video of you sharing your expert advice on something. Send the video off to a subtitling firm such as rev.com, then post.

That's one piece of content.

Tweak the subtitle text into a blog. Now you have two pieces of content.

Reduce the blog into a long-form social media post. Three.

Reduce the blog into a short-form social media post. Four.

Choose two of the best lines from the blog for quote cards. Five and six.

Rip out the audio from the video and use it as a microcast. Seven.

There you go. Seven pieces of content from one video. That's repurposing, and it'll make your life much easier.

## RULE OF THUMB

A good rule of thumb when it comes to social media content is to ask yourself one question: does this **inspire**, **educate** or **entertain**?

Every post you create should do one or more of these three things.

If it doesn't, save yourself the hassle and don't post it.

## WHEN TO POST, WHAT STATS TO CHECK, BLAH, BLAH, BLAH

Without wanting to sound like a scratched record, if you're paying for ads, none of this shit really matters.

Most SMEs stress over the best times to post, what today's reach was vs. yesterday's, how many more numbers can we type into a spreadsheet... And they do this because they want to squeeze as much juice as they can out of social media without having to pay for it.

Of course, you don't want to be posting when no one's online. But you don't want to be posting when everyone's online either, when every other business is fighting for their eyeballs. So yes, do some research. Sometimes, we'll post in the morning. Other times, we post in the evening. Or at the weekend. And do you know what? It doesn't make a blind bit of difference.

**Your organic marketing is there to supplement and complement your paid-for marketing.** We will go into this in detail in Step 9.

Maybe this is even the no.1 rule of marketing.

Make sure your social media numbers are going up – or at least not steadily declining. But I'm talking about a once-a-month task here. Look at your reach and engagement primarily. How many individuals have seen your content and how many have interacted with it? <u>Key</u> metrics. Which posts have worked well? Which haven't? *Do more of the former next month. Meeting over.*

What kills many a business is *paralysis by analysis*. They can't see the wood for the trees. If my organic reach has gone down but sales have gone up, guess what? I don't give a shit!

This is the harsh reality that fluffy marketers can't hack because it would put them out of a job.

## DO OR DO NOT

It's that bloody Yoda again.

If you're going down the social media route, commit to it or don't bother. If you can't post a variety of content across two or three platforms five to 10 times a week, focus on some other kind of marketing.

Also, people make snap judgements. They see that you're on Facebook, they go and check out your page and see that you last posted two weeks ago. It's like having a news page on your website and your last piece of news is six months old. That's a common one. You'd be better off *not* having a news page.

Without consistency, you won't get enough meaningful interaction and traction off those who matter.

It's lovely when your friends come and like your Facebook Page or connect with you on Linky Dink, but that's vanity marketing. They're not going to buy off you! (Well, they might but they'll probably want a big discount.) You want to reach and engage with people you don't know, to strike up a relationship with them and make them more likely to buy from you.

So the next time you get annoyed because a competitor's post gets lots of likes, tell yourself they're probably from his/her mum's sewing circle.

Do you know what "likes" stands for?

Lazy Icons Keeping Everyone Stuck.

Beware of any marketer who tries to sell you likes. They're nice to have but they won't pay the bills.

In a nutshell, your social media has to look cool from the off and show recent, regular posts. There's no point putting social media icons on your business cards and leaflets when what people find may do more harm than good. Don't wear them like a badge of pride when all they're doing is highlighting weak areas in your business. People don't want to see that. Again, they'll make a snap judgement.

They don't care that you're working 80 hours a week to feed your family. They just see an Instagram account that was last posted on a month ago and assume *you* don't care. This assumption may be wrong, but it's powerful.

When people see your ad somewhere, they'll go and check out your website and/or your socials. Both need to impress. Otherwise, you've just wasted your money.

Even though our Marketing That Sells™ system is driven by paid-for ads, it is underpinned by organic social media. Trust us, it is!

Your social media is there to seal the deal. That's how you should look at it. When your competitors are treating it as a bit of fun, "because it's free" and "an eight-year old could do it", just smile to yourself.

# STEP 5

BY JOEL STONE

# STEP 5

## CONSIDER WHAT THIS IS ALL THIS WORTH TO YOU

BY JOEL STONE

Most businesses don't know the value of their customers.

We repeat, <u>most businesses don't know the value of their customers</u>.

Let that sink in for a second…

Sounds like madness, doesn't it? But think about it. You probably spend so much time trying to keep customers happy, chasing new customers and dealing with other issues that you've never stopped to think about your customer's true value.

And it matters! It really matters! If you don't know what a customer is worth, you'll never know what you'd be willing to invest to acquire that customer.

An HR software company approached us once, wanting some help with winning new business. Derek (he wasn't called Derek) thought their marketing budget was huge and he couldn't understand why his subscriber base wasn't growing at the speed he expected.

Derek's software business had proven quite lucrative. He'd been making a nice living for him and his family, and his small, yet efficient team kept the software up to date with the latest changes in HR. The problem was that the business had plateaued. Year-on-year turnover was pretty much stagnant.

Their customers were loyal. In fact, customers stayed with them for around four years, at which point they probably went on to buy bespoke software. Derek knew most of his customers, as they had come from years of networking up and down the county and from various expos.

It confused Derek that his monthly marketing budget of £10,000 seemed to make little to no difference to his business. He was only gaining a couple of customers a month. Everything he'd ever read said he needed to market his business. He was sure they were targeting the right people, with the right language, on the right platforms, and his website was spot on.

So why wasn't he seeing significant customer growth?

We sat Derek down and asked him a series of questions. The conversation went something like this…

Us: *How many new customers do you need per month to achieve your goals?*

Derek: *A minimum of 15.*

Us: *And what is a customer worth to you?*

Derek: *Our current fees are £500 per month.*

(That was when we knew for sure that Derek didn't know the value of a customer. But more on that later!)

Us: *And how long does a customer stay with you?*

Derek: *On average, just over four years. Then they usually need a bespoke system.*

There are a couple of things we can calculate from this information. If you like maths, you'll love this bit. If you don't like maths, you still need to hear it!

## CUSTOMER LIFETIME VALUE

Purchase value × number of purchases in a year × years a customer = lifetime value of a customer

In Derek's case… £500 × 12 × 4 = £24,000

<u>The value of customers acquired in any given period</u>

Customer Lifetime Value × customers acquired in the period

In Derek's case, he wanted a minimum of 15 customers per month…

£24,000 × 15 = £360,000

Wait. What? £360,000 worth of customers acquired every month?!

Have you spotted the issue?

Derek was spending £10,000 per month attempting to acquire £360,000 worth of custom. A return of £36 for every £1 spent.

If you find a business with that kind of marketing ROI, let us know. We want a slice of their business!

Like most businesspeople, Derek hadn't looked at it like that. In his mind, he was trying to bring in an extra £7,500 per month off a marketing spend of £10,000. It felt like he was losing on his investment.

## HOW DEREK AND MOST BUSINESS OWNERS THINK (THE WRONG WAY)

Transactional value of customer × customers acquired in the period = new business

New business − the marketing budget for that period = return on investment

In Derek's case…

£500 × 15 = £7,500
£7,500 − £10,000 = -£2,500

Blimey, no wonder Derek felt annoyed!

As you can now imagine, this was an eye-opening interaction for Derek. A 20-minute chat had given him a completely different view of things.

It turned out that those two customers he brought in each month had a total lifetime customer value of £48,000. For every £10,000 he was investing in his marketing, he was getting nearly five times back.

It took 20 minutes to go from "my marketing is failing" to "my marketing is bloody awesome, thanks very much".

If you always think in transactional terms, you'll always have a transactional business. Do you want to acquire customers for the long term, or do you only want them to buy from you once?

So, what does this mean for you?

Whether you own a hair salon or you're a solicitor, each of your customers has a lifetime value. You'll know how much you're willing to spend to acquire that customer based on how much they're worth to you.

And this is where it gets really interesting...

## HOW MANY CUSTOMERS
## WOULD YOU LIKE?

Once you know how much it costs you to acquire a customer, you can choose how many customers you want.

Whoa. Imagine that. The power to choose how many customers you have. And further still, the ability to turn that volume up or down.

How about a hair salon example? An industry that's a good demonstration of how knowing your Customer Lifetime Value works for a business with a different customer model.

Tracey owns a hair salon. Tracey knows that the average transaction is worth £80. Her regular customers visit the salon six times a year.

Tracey has been in the hairdressing business a while. When someone becomes a customer, they don't tend to leave. But she does get some one-off jobs and jobs like wedding hair and special events. On average, a customer remains a customer for at least 10 years.

Let's do the maths…

Purchase value x number of purchases in a year x years a customer = Customer Lifetime Value

£80 × 6 × 10 = £4,800

On that basis, Tracey decides she is willing to spend up to £500 to acquire a new customer. So, she engages a marketing company that pulls together a campaign aimed at getting new people into her salon (the right kind of people, don't forget Step 1).

After a month, and with a budget of £1,500 per month, Tracey has six new customers. This pattern continues for six months.

## CUSTOMER ACQUISITION COST

Sales and marketing budget / customers acquired = Customer Acquisition Cost

£1,500 / 6 = £250

Tracey now has proof that it costs her £250 to acquire the right kind of customer (Step 1). Now she can literally choose how many customers she wants.

But (of course there is a but) you do have to apply some common sense here. Whether you're a salon, a car dealership or a personal trainer, you have to make a judgement on the size of your audience.

If Tracey's salon is in London, she has a huge number of people to target. If her salon is in a rural village 20 miles from the nearest town, it's a different prospect altogether.

# THE BONUS BIT

What if, for every three customers Tracey acquires, one of them refers someone else to her salon? Instead of acquiring six new customers, she acquires eight. Six paid for through her marketing and two acquired through the great service provided by her team and word of mouth.

In Tracey's case, that would mean that for every £1,500 she invests in marketing, she's acquiring £38,400 in customer value. In one month!

And in Derek's case?

We introduced a referral scheme. If an existing customer introduces a new customer to the HR software, both parties get entered into a prize draw for an iPad.

For every 15 customers acquired, Derek got two referrals. A further £48,000 in customer value for no additional investment (apart from the few quid it cost us to set up and run the competition).

Remember, most businesses don't know the value of their customers – that includes your competitors. But now you've got the formulas to steal a run off everyone!

Just so we're crystal clear, here they are again:

Customer Lifetime Value
Purchase value × number of purchases in a year × years a customer = lifetime value of a customer

The value of customers acquired in any given period
Lifetime value of a customer × customers acquired in the period

Customer Acquisition Cost
Sales and marketing budget / customers acquired = customer acquisition cost

With these three simple calculations, you have the insight and knowledge to judge exactly how much you're willing to spend on acquiring a customer, how many customers you want and how quickly you want them.

Powerful stuff, eh?

"Hang on, but what if my marketing campaign is awful and wastes all my budget?" Well, that's why you need to go through <u>all</u> the steps in this book....

STAY HUNGRY

MARKETING DELIVERED

✦ CODEBREAK

# STEP 6

## BY ANDY RAO

# STEP 6

# WORK OUT WHAT'S IN IT FOR THEM

### BY ANDY RAO

All people want to know when they see a piece of marketing is, **"What's in it for me?"**

## PERMANENTLY TUNE INTO WII FM

There are people out there who will buy off you because you're local. Or because you have a young family. Or because you love dogs. But they're a rare breed (no pun intended). The key thing is that you can't *expect* someone to buy off you because of any of the above. Entitlement is rife and the downfall of many a business.

"Buy your book from me because I'm a local bookstore!"

"I can sit on my backside and order the book from Amazon for half the price and get it delivered to me free the next day."

If you want people to buy from your local bookstore, you need to give them a reason. Start selling coffee. Create a reading area. Get authors in for book signings. If you simply believe you're *entitled* to people's money, you won't be around for long. It's a cruel world, I know.

In all the marketing you do, a guiding principle has to be empathy with your target demographic. Put yourself in their shoes. What's in it for them?

## HAVE FUN

Our social media content rule is a good place to start. Remember? Does the piece of marketing you're about to do <u>inspire, educate or entertain</u>? It has to tick one or more of these boxes first.

Even if you've just made them smile, that's still entertaining them. And that's what's in it for them. Perhaps they were having a crappy day and you've just come along and cheered them up. Now they'll be more likely to like and remember you.

Then they'll be more likely to buy off you.

You'll see lots of the big boys engaging in social media banter with their competitors. Tesco having a laugh with Sainsbury's, KFC giving Burger King a cuddle, and so on. It's a quick way to make their content go viral, but they ain't doing it because they're lovely and funny and sweet. They're doing it to get your buy-in. They're doing it to SELL.

Understand the importance of fun.

Now, for all I know, you could be a Will writer. Not much fun in that game, talking about death and people's kids missing out on their fortune. In your case, no, you're not going to be cracking funnies – but you still have to stand out. Be different. And certainly educate and/or inspire.

How have you helped your existing clients? That's what's in it for people who aren't yet clients. Scare the shit out of them once in a while with a true horror story. Remember that people would rather avoid pain than seek pleasure.

But, generally, most small to medium-sized businesses can inject some informality into the proceedings. If you're in a stuffy industry, the world's your oyster. It should be easy to stand out, to grab people's attention and then hook them.

## THOU SHALT HAVE A FISHIE

So you've got someone's attention. The right someone. The someone most likely to buy off you. With all the noise, dross and lazy marketing out there, your ad or leaflet or email has stood out. Job no.1 done.

Now you've got to reel them in, or at least start the process.

There are two main ways of doing this: via a **special offer** or a **lead magnet**.

You've got to give before you receive. Not that we're massive hippies who believe that the universe will repay you for all the goodness that you put out there... But we definitely believe you have to give first. Or, rather, that's what the numbers have shown us over the years!

What's in it for them? A deal or discount? Or a free guide perhaps? That's what we're talking about. And it doesn't matter how premium you are. Walk into a Ferrari showroom and you'll get some kind of deal. No business is above a deal. And everybody wants one. Or think they're getting one. It doesn't matter, as long as they're happy.

Ultimately, offers and lead magnets are ways of getting more people onto your database. Not forgetting that an offer will also get you that immediate cash hit. However, offers aren't the right fit for every business at the outset. A lead magnet might suit you better. (More of that in a bit.)

## SPECIAL OFFERS

We've generated millions of pounds for clients thanks to special offers. It's that simple. Even a straightforward, boring "% off" deal.

Not that a percentage off should be your first port of call, although it *is* the easiest if you've got the margins to allow for it. A "% off" deal falls into the aforementioned vanilla-like marketing category. But, hey, if it works, so be it. Test and measure, baby. Test and measure.

Let's have an example. There's a blinds business we've helped many a time. Basically, every time this client is quiet, we run a "10% off" ad campaign for him and the orders start flying in. There's no rhyme or reason to it. It actually goes against our marketing principles. But we mustn't be precious. Client sales come first!

Offers work best when they come with deadlines, unless it's an offer to get someone onto your mailing list. In other words, an offer you're going to be running for the foreseeable.

If it's an offer to sell something *now*, where the goal isn't to get people onto your list, again, you need to "force" the person to take action. A deadline helps with that.

No deadline? They'll get onto it tomorrow. A deadline far into the future? Same result. So be tighter with your deadline. Today, tomorrow, this week, this month... Anything longer than one month and it may as well be next year – there's no impetus for the person to sort it out now. They'll leave it for later, and by then, a hundred things will have gotten in the way. Shopping, kids' homework, an unexpected bill, fixing that wonky shelf... You'll be low down on their priority list.

A good deal has to be clear and compelling. "Do it and do it now." Life really will get in the way otherwise.

We're not fans of the hard sell at Codebreak, but we've been around the block enough times to know that hard selling still exists because it works. Yes, it's a numbers game. Yes, you've got to be tough-skinned. But what you end up with at the end of the conversation is a yes or a no. Move on accordingly. Limbo Land is not a nice place to be.

"I'll think about it" is a slow no.

## BE CREATIVE!

The best offers are the creative ones. The big boys can do it well. Here in the UK, the likes of Sainsbury's and Boots are two of the best at running offers. Offers that add value. Offers that give you a deal. You're still spending more.

Let's look at some examples…

Spend £X and get Y free.

3 for 2.

Spend £X and get Y% off.

Spend X and enjoy free delivery.

You go into the shops to get some toothpaste, but come out with toothpaste, mouthwash and dental floss. You want one prawn masala meal, but you come away with three…

We've got to stress this again – and don't laugh and think this is beneath you. YOU NEED TO HOOK THEM FISHIES IN.

You're close to dropping a tonne of money on a new car. It's a lot of money to spend each month, but it's sweeeeeeeet. You're on the edge. What do you do? Then the salesperson says they'll chuck in free floor mats and a yearly service and BINGO! SOLD! (Similarly, if you're about to spend a lot of money on something, don't be afraid to ask for something extra to be included… as long as you're prepared to walk away.)

B2C use offers. B2B use offers. We've even seen big legal firms use offers. "Get your Lasting Power of Attorney done with us, and we'll do your partner's for half price!"

There WILL be some kind of deal you can do in your business.

Some deals can be seasonal too. The whole Black Friday/Cyber Monday thing is huge now, but depending on your industry, there are loads of other times of the year you may be able to capitalise on. Gyms will always do something for New Year. They know people are feeling sluggish after Christmas. Then you've got Valentine's Day, Spring, Easter, Father's Day, Summer… you name it.

Just make sure your offer stands out against those of competitors. If all your competitors run offers like "10% off", you need to be at a different party. You may even want to consider a loss-leading offer.

## LOSS LEADERS

If you sell a widget for £10 and the profit is £2, it sounds like madness to run a 50% off deal. But if your widget is good and one that people need to buy again and again, it might not be so silly.

Let's say you sell tubs of bird nuts for £10, and it's 50% off your first tub. So you lose money on selling that first tub. But, if you're smart and keep in touch with that buyer via email, retargeting and social, they'll buy a second tub the following month at full price. And the same for month three, month four, ad infinitum...

Suddenly, your loss-leading offer is the best thing since sliced bread. The risk is there's only one way to test it. And that's to, er... test it. It will either work or it won't. If you haven't got your relationship marketing right (how you stay in touch with people once they've bought your product/service), it won't work, just to be clear. Nail that down first.

Don't make the mistake of being complacent with your customers. Ever.

It's said that it costs eight times more money to acquire a new customer than it would to keep hold of an existing one. Happy customers will buy off you again and again and **refer you to their friends**. Easy money, right?

Also, people who get referred will be similar to the people who referred them. Because we hang around with people like ourselves. From a commercial perspective, this means referrals are unlikely to be a pain in the arse. Wonderful! So, look after your happy customers. Make sure you're giving them regular cuddles. Everyone loves a cuddle. Some might say now more than ever.

Life's too short to deal with pains in the arse. The customer is always right? BOLLOCKS! The customer is only right when you're not delivering what you promised.

## LEAD MAGNETS

You want more leads. But that won't happen by magic.

"Sign up for my newsletter." Yawn. Why should I? What's in it for me?

So you dangle an offer in front of them, they take you up on it, you make some money *and* have a new person on your database. Winner, winner, chicken dinner.

But, say you're a management consultant. You probably can't steam into a cold lead with a special offer. That comes further on down the line, when they're interested and you need to get them over the line.

*Always* have something you can pull out of the bag to get them over the line.

Be prepared. Don't try and work something out on the spot when you're in the middle of negotiating. You might live to regret it and realise the profit isn't what it needs to be because of what you offered.

In this case, to get a cold lead onto your database, a lead magnet would be more suitable. Like a handy PDF that people are happy to give their email address for. Sound advice from an expert in their field. Yes, you! Your ad drives people to a landing page, they get wowed by your copywriting genius, fill out the form and you've got 'em. They're in your funnel.

(More on ads and funnels later.)

## THE MONEY'S IN THE DETAIL

Your PDF should be honest and detailed. No one likes being conned.

If you're promising "Five Exercises At Home To Lose Weight In A Month", then that's what you deliver. A decent amount of info on these five exercises; not a few bullet points. Not a PDF that says you actually need to spend £1,000 on a home gym. Not only will this lose you a potential customer, but they'll probably badmouth you publicly the next time they see one of your ads. Or leave you a scathing review. Or both.

By the same token, you don't want to talk yourself out of a sale either. Share your juicy tips and insights <u>but</u> make it clear that to get the full benefit or take things to the next level, they need to become a customer of yours.

The PDF's job is to position you as the go-to business in your industry. You know your shit. You need to convey trust and friendliness in your writing, backed up of course by customer testimonials. Identify pain points and how those pains can be solved.

We're not necessarily talking *War and Peace*, but something that prints off on two sides of A4 may leave people feeling a bit cheated. If writing ain't your bag, either pay a professional or test whether a video would cut it. Share your top tips on a cool video. There could be a market for that.

Whether it's a PDF that people view and/or print or a video, it must ooze <u>quality</u>. If your PDF looks like it was designed by a four-year old with a pack of crayons, people won't get past page one. So put some thought into this. Don't be tempted to cram every square inch with content; space it out. Space is good when it comes to design. Think Apple.

Getting a piece of marketing to the point where you're 90% satisfied is a solid benchmark. We've found that when you're targeting 100% satisfaction (in most pieces of marketing), it never actually gets signed off. A sales letter that's 90% there will work harder for you when it's being delivered vs. the sales letter that's still in your drawer waiting for round 50 of amends.

## HIGH BARRIER TO ENTRY

The awesome thing about lead magnets is that not many businesses do them, or they certainly don't do them well.

A good lead magnet is a high barrier to entry. If something requires a fair amount of money and/or effort, it will stop most people from doing it. So, if you're the business in your industry that *can* be bothered, happy days. You're going to provide a free PDF that looks great and shares expert insights that will genuinely help the reader.

A few businesses will actually give away a hard copy PDF, or some, even a book. A free book! That takes some guts, but it will sure set you apart. One of Codebreak's own PDF lead magnets is

13,000 words, and we toyed with the idea of getting it properly printed and stapled... but nah. We decided it wouldn't impact results enough.

Generally speaking, keeping everything <u>online</u> is easier and more cost effective. If the recipient wants to print off your PDF, then that's up to them.

Once you've got their email address, send them to a "thank you" webpage and send the PDF via email. Email no.1 in your funnel is all about affirming what a smart decision they've made and delivering the goods. Simple. You don't want to confuse matters by launching into a pitch or talking about anything else. It's all about the PDF you're giving away because you're so lovely.

Many businesses race in with a hard sell here. DON'T!

If you want to make some kind of sale, do it on the "thank you" page. That's pretty common. We do it ourselves sometimes.

"You've requested our free PDF but did you know we're also selling XYZ which will further help you..."

What you're selling here should be low cost, a nice bonus if it comes in but nothing you're that fussed about. The ideal result is that it generates enough to pay for the ads.

Ads, funnels... both AMAZING when implemented correctly. And, handily, that's what the next two steps in this guide are about.

MARKETING DELIVERED

CODEBREAK

# STEP 7

## BY JOEL STONE

# STEP 7
# SPECULATE TO ACCUMULATE
BY JOEL STONE

Marketing That Sells™ doesn't work without advertising. Sure, you can drive a marketing campaign through blood, sweat and tears. You can spend every waking moment finding prospects, cold calling, cold emailing, chasing and asking for referrals, but is that the best use of your time?

No. The answer is no.

If you *can* pay to drive profitable custom towards your business, it should be a no brainer.

If you're currently running your marketing campaigns without any form of paid advertising driving them, you're fighting with one hand tied behind your back.

If you're in business, chances are you've tried advertising before. And if that's the case, there's just as much chance that you've been burnt by advertising too.

In the wrong hands, advertising can be a quick way to burn through money. And worse still, you could burn through all that cash and have nothing to show for it.

There is a better way.

## INVESTMENT NOT A COST

The majority of SME business owners built their businesses through hard graft. To get their business off the ground, they pulled in favours and they worked all hours. They went to the opening of an envelope, and there's no shame in that. No shame at all. Most of us don't have a huge loan or trust fund to see us through the first few years.

However, when the business starts to see some traction, the smart business owners know how to take things to the next level. And the good news is, it's a simple step in the Marketing That Sells™ process.

Let's say you meet us in the street and we say, "For every £1 you give us, we'll give you £2 back". You would beg, borrow and steal to find as much money as you could. That's the mentality you need to have with your advertising.

Think about the steps you've read about so far in this book. You know exactly who your customer is and you know what they're worth to you. Because you know all that, you also know what you're willing to spend to acquire that kind of customer.

With that knowledge alone, advertising should already feel far less intimidating.

Your perspective should have shifted. You're no longer thinking about spending your marketing budget in any given month and seeing what return you get that same month. You should be thinking about the customer value that spend is going to bring you over time.

So then, what if you had a situation where for every £50 you spent, you got a certain number of leads. And then for every 10 leads, you get two enquiries. And for every two enquiries, one becomes a customer…

Remember Tracey, the salon owner? Once she did the maths, she could literally choose how many customers she had. The fuel for that fire was advertising.

In the Marketing That Sells™ system, the initial goal of advertising is to gather data. Your offer (Step 6) should be attractive enough that your target customer is willing to swap their details for it.

## TAKING CONTROL

The mistake most businesses make is going for the kill too soon. This is a sure-fire way to burn through your budget. If the aim of your initial adverts is to secure a sale, that's just as bad as proposing on the first date. *Cringe.*

The best part of taking a data-first approach is it puts you in control. Once you have a potential customer's contact details, you can choose how to contact them in the future. You're no longer solely reliant on Facebook, LinkedIn, Google, the local newspaper, or whatever platform is driving your interest.

And once you've got those details, you can begin the process of warming that prospect up towards a sale. (More on that later!)

Any initial ads should drive people to take action that means you can carry on communicating with them forevermore (unless they unsubscribe, but hardly anybody does).

That could be something as simple as a cookie or a pixel so you can remarket to them, or it might be them leaving their details behind and going into your marketing funnel.

Oh damn, technobabble! The only cookies you care about are the ones you eat and the only pixels you've heard of are the mega ones on your phone camera.

The Marketing That Sells™ system focuses on using Facebook Ads or Google Ads initially (or a combination of both). Let's work through all the advertising (and tracking) need-to-know fundamentals before you get your ads in place.

## FACEBOOK ADS

Facebook Ads is Facebook's advertising platform (no shit).

But, as mentioned earlier, many people are unaware that their ads don't just display on the Facebook newsfeed… they display on Instagram, Marketplace (a bit like Facebook's version of eBay), Facebook Video, Facebook Messenger, Facebook Stories, and Audience Network.

Audience Network extends your advertising reach *beyond* Facebook's own platforms and to places like mobile apps and mobile websites.

Facebook offers a variety of ad objectives. The sexiest to most is the mighty conversion ad. Where you can tell how much it has cost you to do whatever it is you want them to do, e.g. fill out a form, make an enquiry or buy something.

Facebook Ads are *pushed* to the audiences you specify. They don't have to be searched for to be shown. You're using your knowledge to proactively get in front of the people most likely to buy.

## GOOGLE ADS

The Google Ads platform allows advertisers to bid to display brief advertisements, product listings or videos to internet users. Not only can it place ads on Google Search, but on websites and apps too. People refer to this kind of advertising as Google pay-per-click.

At this stage, you should be focusing on Google Search Network adverts.

Google Search Network ads are those ads that display at the top of a Google search. They rely on matching the search terms inputted by the user.

## TRACKING MAGIC

You can track people by cookies and pixels and remarket to them. More of this in Step 8. If you tell someone about remarketing when they didn't already know, it's like you've invented fire.

Cookies (sorry, not the food kind)

*Stomach growls*

A cookie is a small piece of data the web browser stores on the user's computer while they browse a website. In Google's case, it can be used to track user behaviour on your website – what pages they visit, how long they spend on them, and so on.

Pixels (not the camera kind)

Facebook's cookie equivalent. Again, used to track user behaviour on your website and feed that information back to Facebook.

There's no point building an ad campaign unless you can track it. What are these people doing, where are they going and how do I get them to remember me…? That's why you need to know about cookies and pixels.

## BUILDING YOUR FACEBOOK ADS

Build an audience based on your target customer.

Think back to Step 1. All that thought and research is about to pay off!

With Facebook, you can build an audience based on location, gender, interests, employment and various other factors. You can also narrow your audiences using these factors too.

If your customer is a British, high achieving, young professional, then perhaps your audience would look like this:

Location: lives in London

Age: 19 to 30

Interested in: Harvey Nichols, Selfridges, cocktails, reading, current affairs

Must also be interested in (the narrowing factor): socialising, FTSE, Bitcoin

Now if you're selling low-cost walking boots in the UK, perhaps your audience would look a little bit more like this:

Location: lives in the UK

Age: 16 to 70

Interested in: Aldi, Lidl, Matalan, Sports Direct

Must also be interested in (the narrowing factor): rambling, the outdoors, walking holidays

Facebook uses this information to serve your adverts to the right people. Trust us, Facebook knows a lot about people, including you. This might sound creepy, but it's true. It's where we need to put our 'Business Owner' hats on.

You know that feeling you get when you think Facebook has been listening to you? You open up Facebook and an advert is served to you about something you have literally just been chatting about. You start glancing around the room like someone's watching you…. (Don't watch *The Invisible Man* (2020) if this makes you shiver!)

The same triggers that caused you to talk about it are the triggers around the internet and in your social media behaviour that Facebook is monitoring. It's actively learning people's interests based on their online behaviour. And you can use it to your business's advantage. You're literally serving people content that they want to see.

The objective of your adverts is to drive people to a landing page to capture their data or capture their data directly. In return, they'll get your giveaway (Step 6). Remember, this could be a freebie, it could be an offer or it could be exclusive access. Whatever it is, it has to be valuable enough to be worth swapping some details for.

We always build our ads with a variety of headlines, descriptions and images. This allows us to test and measure (more on that later) what the audience responds to most. Then we can adjust and tweak our campaigns accordingly.

There are three key elements to any Facebook ad; the visual, the text and the call to action.

The visual is made up of an eye-catching image or a mustwatch video that quickly demonstrates your offer or the problem you're solving.

The text is where you get to the point. Your opening line should directly address your offering and make it clear. People skim read, so use the headline to grab their attention. The text and image should complement each other.

The call to action is the little button that reads "Sign up" or "Learn more" or "Download", etc. Choose the call to action that aligns with your campaign. "Learn more" will generally fit most campaigns if you're driving traffic to a landing page.

## GETTING FOUND FOR THE RIGHT SEARCHES

Google Search Network ads are the other way to go about getting people added to your list. These rely on displaying your website and a brief description to people who have searched using terms relating to your campaign.

If you're giving away a free guide on how to maintain your lawn, people might search "free lawn maintenance guide" or "how to maintain my grass" or "make my lawn better".

Think about what people might Google if they're looking for your giveaway. You should also think about all the things people might search that you DON'T want to show for. This is important too.

Using the above example, a company giving away a lawn maintenance guide won't want searches like "replace my lawn" or "add paving slabs to my lawn", etc. However, those phrases do contain the word "lawn". You need to be smart. It's just as important to tell Google what you don't want as what you do want. Otherwise, you'll burn through your budget in no time and have a lot less people added to your list.

Go back to Step 1 and your ideal customer. What kind of things do they search for? What is the problem they're trying to solve? What do they want a discount on?

You can also restrict your search ads by location. If you can only help people in the UK or your region, there's no point serving search ads beyond this locale.

You thought you were being smart, didn't you? When you were

finding those free guides or searching for voucher codes. That's what those companies wanted you to do, so it's a win-win for all involved.

With Google Search Network, you are bidding on the value of the search terms. The more competitive the search term, the more it will cost you. This is another reason to know your niche.

Think about it this way. "Replace my wooden windows" will be a less competitive search term than "replace my windows". Or (and this is if you're really specialist), "replace my half Georgian wooden windows" will be even less competitive and therefore cost less again. If you only manufacture half Georgian wooden windows (seems unlikely but you get the point), why bother bidding on search terms that cost you more and have you competing with businesses that aren't even offering the same thing?

Nail down what your target customer would search for and discount anything that will waste your budget.

Your headline and description should relate to the search query you're targeting. If someone has searched for a "free lawn maintenance guide", the headline should be "free lawn maintenance guide". The description should add a little more flesh to the bones… "Transform your lawn from a desolate wasteland into a luscious, green paradise with our easy-to-follow, free guide."

Perhaps not quite so exaggerated, but you get the idea.

Has the user found what they were looking for? How will it solve their problem?

## WHAT DO YOU SPEND?

And that just leaves your budget. You can set your budget based on daily spend or lifetime spend. You know what you're willing to spend to acquire a customer and you know how many customers you want. You should, therefore, have set a marketing budget.

A large proportion of that budget will be spent on your initial ads. These are the ads to get people in at the top of your marketing funnel (jargon speak for filtering down to the people most likely to buy).

This is where most ad campaigns fall down. Most businesses test with a tiny budget to "see if this shit works". And guess what? It never does. They reinforce their "I told you so" beliefs and revert back to their old way of doing things.

Neither Facebook nor Google works like that. These are advertising marketplaces. If you're not willing to bid what a customer is worth, you can forget it. You'll never acquire them.

The old school equivalent is having a double-page spread in a popular magazine vs having a 1/8th black and white ad in amongst the classified ads at the back. Which one do you reckon gets more attention?

If you want to acquire a customer with a lifetime value to your business of £40,000, don't expect a £100 per month advertising budget to do that for you.

Low margin products or services often require a higher percentage of budget because they need to make a high volume of sales. Whereas high margin products/services are likely to require a smaller percentage. That could still represent a large outlay of cash because, as a high margin product/service, your Customer Lifetime Value will be high.

An easy way to think about this is as follows...

Ferrari's marketing budget as a percentage of their customer value will be less than someone selling an online razor subscription service. Online subscriptions like this regularly spend 40% - 60% of their turnover on marketing. They need volume.

As a prestigious, high-margin brand, Ferrari needs a lot less volume. It wants a specific type of customer, someone who'll be pricey to acquire but, as a percentage of customer value, it will be a lot less than 40%. It does not cost Ferrari £80,000 in marketing budget to help sell a £200,000 car.

Think about how many customers you need in each period, how much each of these will cost to acquire and set your advertising budget accordingly.

Speculate to accumulate.

# STEP 8

BY ANDY RAO

# STEP 8
# MAKE REMARKETING YOUR MISSION

BY ANDY RAO

This chapter is essential reading. Well, OK, they *all* are, really. You know you need *all* the links in the chain to work.

Remarketing is the art of getting in front of people repeatedly. In a nice way. It's a strategy that's as old as the hills but it hasn't always been such a big deal. But then the online world came along and got cluttered... quickly. There was more noise to cut through. People became busier.

If you follow any of Codebreak's socials, you'll know that a favourite phrase of ours is THE WORST NUMBER IN MARKETING IS ONE. It might even be stated in this book five or six times, it's that important.

It would be wonderful if people saw a piece of your marketing once then magically bought off you. But unfortunately, we don't live in Narnia. Sure, you'll make a sale here and there straightaway – if you catch the right person at the right time with the right message. But let's play the odds here.

Most people will see a piece of marketing and, even if it appeals to them, they won't make a decision there and then. They'll think about it. They'll do some research. They'll get it signed off by their mum's second cousin.

We talked about this earlier, but if you've been in business a long time, you'll know the importance of getting a prospect to make a decision sooner rather than later. You may have invested your time into preparing a pitch deck, then driving to the meeting, then having the meeting, which drags on because you didn't take charge early enough and set the parameters... only to have the prospect say to you, "Sounds great. I'll think about it."

They genuinely *may* want to think about it. But that means there's more time for one of your competitors to wheedle their way in there. Once you've left the party, the odds only go down. Now, if only there was a cost-effective way to stay in front of that person and remind them of how much they need you...

## AD RETARGETING

You've always been able to remarket, of course. You could leave your meeting and then send the person some choccies in the post. Or mail them a brochure. Tickets to the opera. Follow up with a couple of emails. The trouble is, that's all manual, it takes a lot of time and probably costs you a bomb.

Using online ads to stay in front of your prospects and, well, anyone who has engaged with your online content is low cost and pretty much automated.

The two main players are Facebook Ads and Google Display Ads. Both work the same way. Someone lands on your website or on a specific page on your website, that fires a pixel or cookie, which allows Facebook/Google to track that person across the internet and serve them ads on other websites. Remember, when you see an ad on a website, chances are it's hosted by Facebook or Google.

Many businesspeople know about ad retargeting. But there are some we talk to about it and it's like we've invented fire. They had no idea *that's* how it works. They may not even have been consciously aware of it. Only when they think back do they realise that the pair of trainers they looked at online is now following them around.

Rarely will we run an ad campaign for a business without including retargeting. Even if the goal is to get people to download a PDF from a landing page, we will retarget those who visited said page but didn't download the PDF.

Buy or die.

Sounds harsh but it's a mantra to bear in mind. As long as you're not doing anything unethical, it's your job to stay in front of (the right) people until they buy from you, say no and/or refer you. You *have* to be OK with this.

If you're a shy, retiring wallflower who wants to talk to somebody once about your product or service that can help them, you need to pay someone else to do your marketing. And that's fine. There's nothing wrong with that. We're all for getting out of comfort zones, but if something like this would create an ever-present state of anxiety, outsource it. That's what lots of people do. It's smart thinking.

As always, the copy in your retargeting ads has to be spot-on. It can't be all stalker-like, e.g. "We know you've looked at our trainers! Buy them now!" You've got to be subtle. Remember, it's easy to make people uneasy and that's not what you want.

"Our 5-star rated trainers are selling fast! Grab yours today with this 15% discount code."

You may not want to run an offer so soon, but it's a sure-fire way of taking someone who's a warm prospect to a hot prospect.

Just be mindful that if you want repeat purchases from someone, if they've got any sense, they'll play this game again and again. They'll never pay full price. They'll look at a product or service on your website and then wait, knowing they'll probably get served an offer code. Which might be fine with you. Take the money!

This goes without saying, but if someone is interested in a specific pair of trainers, you want to drive them back to that specific pair of trainers. Not your general trainers page. Make it easy for them. Always. If they're in exactly the right place, it's easy to enquire or buy. If you are taking money online, make that easy too. If you don't offer PayPal as an option, you'll lose out. There are people who won't have their credit cards saved on their phone and they can't be arsed to get off the sofa to fetch their wallet.

Lastly, note that retargeting ads tend to be more expensive than "normal" clicks-to-website ads. As ever, do the maths. (More on testing and measuring in Step 10.)

## LANDING PAGES

Before we leap into the world of remarketing by email, let's have a quick look at landing pages.

Every business should have at least one landing page. A webpage where there is a single call to action and nowhere else for the visitor to go. No links to other webpages. *Choice is bad.*

We used to love choices here at Codebreak. It's good to give people a choice, right?

Nope.

Choices create indecision, and once people start dithering, the chances of them buying drop through the floor.

Have the confidence to know how you can best help someone and present them with that. You may wish to make your call to action "stronger", by presenting what we call a dummy offer alongside it. This reaffirms why they need to go for what you want them to go for.

Let's look at an example. You want to sell someone a hair cream and hairbrush set for £20. Say you anchor that price by offering just the hair cream for £17. Suddenly, your hair cream and hairbrush price looks much more attractive.

Typically, a landing page is where you want to sell one thing or give one thing away, usually a PDF as mentioned earlier. You have ads running that drive people to this page and they either buy, fill out the form or do nothing at all. That's it.

You could host your landing page on your own domain, but make sure you strip out the main navigation menu – again, so they can't go anywhere else. You may need to have the page on your website as normal, (this allows anyone else who's browsing your site to buy or enquire), but don't *pay* to drive people to the webpage we're talking about. Replicate the page either as a hidden page on your website or...

...we'd recommend using a specialist landing page provider instead.

In the numerous tests we have run, driving people to a specialist landing page is more cost effective than driving people to a hidden page on your own domain. We can only assume there are some brown envelopes being passed around. Regardless, we follow the numbers. If it costs you less to get people to a specialist landing page, who are we to argue?!

There's a tonne of specialist landing page providers to choose from, all pretty much the same. You'll probably be familiar with names such as Clickfunnels and Fastpages.

Some people like long landing pages containing lots of info. Others go for short 'n' sweet. Either way, they have to look cool, identify people's pain, solve that pain and back up their credentials with some testimonials.

When the visitor does what you want them to do, they get taken to a "thank you" page. You may want to offer them a cheeky upsell at this point. But, basically, you're just telling them they're smart for making a great choice. And this URL enables you to run retargeting ads, i.e. those who visited the landing page URL, but not the "thank you" page URL.

This person is now in your database and you should stay in touch with them.

## EMAIL FUNNELS

Another way of remarketing is to run an email funnel. You get the details of people who are interested in what you're selling and they go into an automated sequence of emails.

If you sell a wide range of products or services, this won't be as specific as ad retargeting unless you go down the route of running multiple funnels. This will take a lot more time upfront compared to setting up multiple retargeting ads. You have to make a decision on that. But if you can handle the running and monitoring of multiple email funnels, go for it.

Let's say you run a garden centre and someone is interested in sheds. This strategy will allow you to send him/her emails about sheds. Not garden hoses or wheelbarrows; sheds. This makes the selling of a shed more likely.

BUT… if they're interested in sheds, they're probably interested in other garden items too. This means that by running <u>one</u> email funnel, a more generic one, you could cross-sell more easily. And you'll save – ahem – a shed-load of time.

So it's a tough call and it would come down to your capacity and knowing your audience.

We run funnels for businesses that last a year. The minimum we recommend is two months. An email funnel is a slow burn marketing channel and again, once the front-loaded work is done, it's out there pushing your business without you having to do much.

Here's a trick: at the end of your funnel, set an automation to send recipients through into a general e-newsletter list. Whether that's emailing your database once a month, once a week, whatever… you stay in touch with them.

Again, buy or die.

It goes without saying that your existing customers should be receiving these e-newsletters too. Or perhaps, once someone has made a purchase, they go into another automated funnel. The world's your oyster. Going after prospects and warming them up is common sense, but so is staying in touch with people who may buy again and/or refer you.

## EMAIL FREQUENCY

We're fans of sending emails once a week at least. If that's too rich for you, fortnightly is a good compromise. Once a month? Some might say that's not enough. There's too much opportunity for your competitors to occupy front-of-mind space where *you* should be.

There are still businesses that send out quarterly emails. Four emails a year? You're wasting your time.

If you have a problem with it, email frequency is something you'd benefit from getting over. If you think sending an e-newsletter more than once a month is too much, reconsider.

Do your research. This will serve you better than asking friends. We love our friends, but if they're not successful in business, their (well-meaning) thoughts are irrelevant. Most of Joe Public have a problem with e-newsletters, and it's usually because they subscribed to the wrong lists. They're signed up to receive e-news from businesses that don't know how to do it properly and they assume you'll make the same mistakes.

If you send emails that are purely "sell, sell, sell", you're probably asking for trouble. If they get sent once a day or more... you're definitely asking for trouble.

If your emails *are* going to be sales-heavy, space them out and make them entertaining and/or educational. Offer something of value as well as spinning the sell. Perhaps your insights, or industry news that's relevant to the reader. You get the point. The sell always has to be spun; the pain people have and how you solve it.

We've seen a better long-term return for businesses when their primary funnel focus is to – oh, wait, you've seen this before – inspire, educate and/or entertain. Throw in the odd sell, add a cheeky offer to the bottom... but the main angle is to engage with people, so they stay subscribed and remember you. They may not buy today or tomorrow, but who knows, next week or next month... Maybe! Future buyers might not even open all your emails... and that's OK too.

The Fibonacci sequence is a good place to start with frequency:

Email no.1 – Day 0
Email no.2 – 1 day later
Email no.3 – 1 day after that
Email no.4 – 2 days after that
Email no.5 – 3 days after that
Email no.6 – 5 days after that

Email no.7 – 8 days after that
Email no.8 – 13 days after that

Then you stick to one preferred frequency, maybe every five days. Definitely hit them hard early on, then ease off for a bit. Whatever you do, don't send email no.2 ages after email no.1 because you're "worried about being spammy".

We had to get rid of a client who couldn't get his head around this. We stupidly agreed to play it his way, and then he moaned that his funnel wasn't making him any money….

## EMAIL SYSTEM

It's hard to believe in this day and age that you still have businesses sending mass emails to their database using Outlook.

There's no excuse.

"Reply with 'unsubscribe' as the subject header if you don't want to hear from us again."

Possibly the most unprofessional thing you'll ever read. Apart from not actually offering any way of unsubscribing.

You want to use a legally-compliant mass email system. So the emails will still come from your email address, branded up in your colours, but people can unsubscribe from them by pressing a link. The system will not allow you to email them again and you have a paper trail to prove it.

Most decent mass email systems allow you to run automations, which is your funnel.

## EMAIL STRUCTURE

With all the emails in your funnel and the ensuing e-newsletters, spend time on the subject header and then pre-header (if that's available, depending on what email system you're using).

There's no point having the best email in the world if no bugger opens the thing. When you see the subject header, "Our Latest Newsletter", in your inbox, you're hardly likely to rush to open it, are you?

Our general advice is to go a bit left-field, ask a question or tag in their first name. Here are some examples:

"I blame Kevin Costner"*

"Have you made this mistake?"

"One for you, Bob"

*This is a genuine subject header we've used a few times. It's based around the idea that lots of businesspeople think that when they launch a business, people will magically flock to them, i.e. "Built it and they will come." If you have no idea what we're talking about, go watch *Field of Dreams*.

Some systems will also allow you to put emojis in the subject header. Don't go crazy, but one or two emojis in the header will certainly make your email stand out when people are scanning down their inbox.

If you can achieve an open rate above 20%, you're doing well. Don't obsess about getting more. As long as the percentage doesn't keep going down, of course. And if you suddenly get lots of unsubscribes, check which email triggered them, and change its content accordingly. There will be something that caused the exodus.

When it comes to the email body, remember the golden rule about writing: keep the sentences and paragraphs short. There are many reasons why James Patterson became the world's bestselling author, and this was one of them. Emails, blogs, web copy… whatever, short 'n' sweet will win out.

Purely from a visual point of view, keeping your copy snappy works. Imagine people are looking at your email on a mobile – which they most likely are – and their entire screen is taken up by one big chunk of text… *Urgh.*

The first bite is with the eye.

We like getting people's first names in the data capture forms we deploy, so we can easily personalise the ensuing emails. "Hi Bob," is a better start to an email than, "Hi there." (As long as your name's Bob, of course.)

Some data capture forms like asking for just your email. No first name, last name, nothing. That's good in terms of getting to the point quickly. People certainly aren't going to fill out a form that has 20 fields. But, you will lose the personal touch. First name, last name, email address. Or at least the first name. Job done.

Should you bother with a title field? No. Do you want to send emails to "Mr Smith" and "Mrs Jones"? This ain't the 1950s. If anyone gets snotty about being addressed by their first name, get outta there. They'll be trouble. They're playing amateur power games. If someone insists you call them by their title and surname, insist they address you likewise.

Knowing their first name also allows you to drop it in throughout the copy rather than just the intro. This is good if your email is long as it helps to retain their attention. It's amazing how many businesses don't know about this one. The reader's name will leap out of any piece of copy.

Last point about email writing...

Whenever possible, write about one thing in one email.

Don't try and flog all your wares. Focus on a single aspect of what you do to help people, and talk about something different in the next email. It's like these "elevator pitches" at networking breakfasts – people try and cram everything they do into those 60 seconds. They'd be much better off talking about one specific thing every time. Audiences just don't have the concentration, whether that's reading or listening.

Email is an underused and underestimated tool in this age of instant messaging. Not many businesses use email well, which gives you an awesome opportunity. And the control lies with you. Those email addresses in your database are YOURS. Not Mark Zuckerberg's or anyone else's. As wonderful as many media platforms are, you want to be in charge. Same with your website. If your web designer holds all the cards and you can't access or change shit, sort that out TODAY.

Most purchasing decisions are made because somehow, somewhere, a brand has gotten into your head. That is rarely achieved by doing something once.

Now and then, an awesome ad might come along that resonates the first time and you buy what it's selling. Apple's *Think Different* creative, for example. But chances are, you'll still be exposed to that ad more than once. AND it will have cost a shit-load of money to make!

STAY HUNGRY

MARKETING DELIVERED

CODEBREAK

# STEP 9
BY JOEL STONE

# STEP 9

# NAIL YOUR
# ORGANIC CONTENT

BY JOEL STONE

Organic content… another oft-used marketing term, we know! When marketers say, "Organic content", they mean <u>any</u> of your content that doesn't have budget behind it.

This could be a social media post, it could be a blog, it might even be PR. If it can be found by searching and didn't cost you a bean, it's organic content.

So what's the problem with most businesses' organic content? It's twee, self-involved and potentially does more harm than good. *Ouch.*

Take a quick scroll down your Facebook or your LinkedIn. How much of that business content (forget the pictures of puppies and kittens) is *genuinely* attracting your interest? You see? The prior statement wasn't so brutal after all.

The Marketing That Sells™ system doesn't use organic content to directly drive sales. You'd need incredible bouts of creativity coupled with infinite amounts of time to get close to what Marketing That Sells™ can do for you with organic content.

Your organic content should <u>supplement</u> your paid-for work. It's there to <u>compliment</u> your campaign. What would somebody think of your business if they checked you out on social media?

You should already be familiar with our favourite content rule of thumb by now. All your organic content should <u>inspire, educate or entertain.</u>

Positioning is key. If you have a brilliant marketing campaign, but your social media is full of drunken pictures of your staff at the last Christmas do, what impression are you giving? If you're a party organiser, that might work, but it's probably not so great for a funeral home.

If someone has seen your ads and perhaps even signed up to your email funnel, what impression do you want to create?

There is no right or wrong answer here. The easiest way to tackle organic content is to be authentic.

If your content looks like it represents someone else, that's no good. And worse still, if it looks like you're trying too hard. People will smell that a mile off.

What genuinely represents you?

Let's look at some real-life examples from brands we've worked with that get this right. And more importantly, how getting it right has impacted their marketing campaigns.

We're proud to work with a really progressive accountancy practice. As a business, they were tired of the age-old stereotypes in their industry and the behaviour "norms" everyone seemed to conform to. Think poorly fitting suits, showing up with a briefcase, spending more time doing your timesheet than actual work and a focus on cutting costs rather than investment. All the usual stereotypes associated with that industry.

James (he isn't called James) had a vision for the business to create a friendly, approachable accountancy practice that doesn't take life too seriously, but still takes numbers and business seriously. A focus on people and ambition, not just reporting.

We knew we wanted to work with these accountants when they used their own networking club to launch their own beer. "BEER, you say?" Exactly! How many accountants have their own beer?!

What's more, they had ambitions of buying their own office and converting it into a shared working space for business and events. It would include a pool table, an arcade machine and in their words, "awesome coffee".

Alongside these lofty ambitions, they wanted to support local charities, grow their team (both in numbers and ability) and make work a fun place to be.

It would have been entirely pointless for their organic content to follow the format of many others in their industry. You know the type. The posts that update you on the latest changes to VAT and when your next tax deadline is. *Yawn.* This stuff wouldn't fit their culture, it wouldn't be authentic and it wouldn't supplement all of their other work.

If they truly were accountants with a difference, they couldn't afford to look like everyone else on their social media.

Their organic content does several things along the 'inspire, educate and/or entertain' line to supplement their marketing:

* Reaffirms their expertise (inspires and educates)

They regularly post video guides and updates on any changes in law or tax rules. These are presented from their cool office and absolutely nobody is wearing a badly fitting suit.

* Shows who they are (inspires and entertains)

It showcases the faces behind the business. What they look like, what they sound like, how approachable they are.

* Showcases their office (inspires and educates)

They have an incredible office. It looks more like a bar than an accountancy practice. Shared working spaces, booths, a pool table, an arcade machine, big screens, a coffee machine, collaborative areas. It's welcoming and inviting.

* Reports on their events (inspires, educates and entertains)

They go above and beyond to host a monthly book club, monthly networking, young professionals' networking, an annual quiz, a Christmas cinema screening and more. All of which features to back up the kind of business they are and attract people to future events.

Also:

<u>Everything is on brand</u>

It all looks, sounds and feels consistent with all of their other marketing and communications. Consistency ensures it's easier to remember. It feels legitimate and makes the content easier to engage with because you trust it. It's familiar.

<u>Social proof</u>

Their organic content demonstrates testimonials and case studies from existing clients. They regularly get great feedback, perfect for showcasing the business to organisations thinking about moving to a different accountancy firm.

Everything they do comes back to <u>authenticity</u>. If they suddenly started wearing suits and referencing the upcoming tweaks to legislation from the ICAEW, their audience would soon switch off.

This wouldn't be a great chapter unless we explain the mistakes that most businesses make with their organic content. And there is a reason they do...

That reason is *vanity metrics*.

Vanity metrics are the bane of marketing. Some would argue they're the bane of society! Plus "vanity metrics" is yet another one of those awful marketing terms.

So, what do we mean by it?

Vanity metrics are any time you find yourself measuring the success of your content based on what it looks like on the surface, rather than the net result.

It's the businesses that fish for likes, but never grow. Or the marketing agencies that tell you you've reached loads of people but can't tell you who these people are. It could be a huge increase in website traffic, but absolutely no difference to enquiries.

## POST WITH <u>PURPOSE</u>

Everyone knows that one person who uses Facebook like some weird hybrid of Google and public counselling. You may be unfortunate and know more than one. They use it to garner attention. You'll have seen the posts, but here are some examples just for laughs...

"Does anyone know a good travel agent?"

"Horrible day at work! Glass of wine needed..."

"Hmm, what to have for dinner tonight. Ideas, anyone?"

These are the sort of posts that create engagement and attention, but with no positive outcome. Attention for attention's sake.

In the business world, you see this all the time too. False authenticity, false professionalism and fake fun.

If your solicitor posts on Instagram or Instagram Stories on Pancake Day, asking what toppings you prefer, does that give you confidence that they're a good solicitor? Does it make them more relatable?

If the same solicitor got their team to do a pancake fundraiser for a local charity and then asked the same question, that's a whole different kettle of fish. That action has depth and personality. It shows they don't take themselves too seriously, whilst supporting a serious cause and allowing their staff to get involved in something fun and purposeful.

Don't just jump on holidays, national days or hashtags. Do it with <u>purpose</u>, do it with <u>reason</u>.

If you were to ask a bunch of strangers what their favourite pancake topping was with absolutely no context, it would be considered weird, right? So why would you do it on social media?

Key things to avoid:

- Posting pictures with no context
- Attention-grabbing posts with no business purpose or justification

- Coming up with stuff purely for social media
- *Anything* that doesn't align with your brand or company values
- Images and video that don't represent the position of your business (if you're a high-end business, don't post a blurry photo)
- Relying on organic posts when a modest advertising budget will have far more impact

There is one other major mistake that so many SMEs make. Assigning the social media to someone in the team who merely *shows an interest*.

Having lots of personal social media interaction is different to professional, commercial content creation. Just because one of your employees with 5,000 Instagram followers demonstrates an interest in your business's social media, doesn't mean they'll do a good job for you.

We're serious! What if you've got Bob from Admin managing your social media? What does that say to the world when they find out?!

## STAFF WHO MEAN WELL

You've got to Step 9 in this book, so you clearly take marketing seriously. You understand how good marketing can be transformational for your business.

So letting Bob run riot as your livelihood's digital voice is unwise. The horror stories we could tell you....

You'll see real life examples all the time (especially now we've mentioned it). Business pages posting things such as, "It's Wednesday! Happy hump day! We're halfway there!" Or "It's Friday at last! Have a great weekend, everyone!".

What does that bilge say to the decision-maker looking at your business?

It's basically saying that the people in your business can't wait to get away from work. What might someone then infer? That perhaps they don't enjoy their jobs? That instead of helping your customers, they're counting down the hours to the weekend. Hardly a good impression for a potential customer or your next superstar recruit, eh?

You'll get engagement from these types of posts, but only from people with the same attitude. People that might buy from you because their boss says they have to. People that might work for you because they think it's the right thing to do. Is that the kind of engagement you want?

Some businesses are brilliant at "warts and all" social media. They have smart people behind their content who are able to self-deprecate, be humorous and still position the brand positively and effectively. Chances are you don't have those people, or you're yet to employ that kind of expertise. Don't make the mistake most businesses make and fish for engagement that means nothing. You won't go viral with your "happy hump day" post and a stolen meme.

In summary, the Marketing That Sells™ system uses organic content to back up the paid-for elements. A rough guide for your time would be 75% on the paid-for, 25% on the organic.

If somebody sees your advertising and comes to check out one of your social media profiles, make sure you have presented the authentic version of your business.

Would that person be more confident to buy from you after seeing it? If the answer is no, your content needs work.

Bloody Bob from Admin!

STAY HIINGRY

MARKETING DELIVERED

CODEBREAK

# STEP 10

BY ANDY RAO

# STEP 10
# TEST AND MEASURE
### BY ANDY RAO

1. Knowing your important numbers is VITAL
2. Knowing all your numbers is PARALYSIS BY ANALYSIS

If you love looking at numbers, go be a Maths teacher! The business owners we know who love being immersed in spreadsheets all have one thing in common (well, two if you count the ill-fitting suits) – their businesses aren't successful.

By "successful", we never mean rolling in loot. It isn't *purely* about the money. If money is your main driver, there are probably employed jobs to suit your skills that will give you more money with less of the hassle and responsibility.

**You want to help people.** If that is your main driver, the money will be a lovely off-shoot of that.

By "successful", we mean doing good work, having more freedom than the common man or woman, and ideally not having to worry about money.

Please note that the richest people in the world worry about money. It's not a problem exclusively for the poor. They worry about losing their money, they worry about other people having even more money… It's sad to see, to be honest.

If you struggle to get your head around the concept of money, go buy Felix Dennis's *How to Get Rich.*

Hopefully, you want to be successful in our sense of the word. And to come back to the original point, that's hard if you're spending all the livelong day analysing every number under the sun. So let us make the job easier for you. It's no crime not to know every number in your business.

You want to know about the numbers that matter. No more, no less.

So which numbers matter? We'll break it down in this chapter for you.

Beware of business owners who talk about their numbers too much. Just like beware of business owners who post 50 times a day on their socials.

## WEBSITE TRAFFIC

As ever, let's start with the final link in the chain. Your website.

Hopefully you've got Google Analytics set up, which is free. This tells you how many visits your website receives, how many unique visits, traffic by page and where that traffic has come from. It's handy stuff and easy to read. There is a tonne of other numbers, but again, we're focusing on the important ones.

You want to be plotting these key metrics over time, so you can always see a snapshot of where you are compared to last month or the same time last year. Shouting, "Yay, we had 10,000 website visits in April!" don't mean shit if in April last year, you had 12,000.

Some people will break the numbers down and look at them weekly, daily, hourly... *Yawn.* Looking at things by month should be enough. *Maybe* weekly, depending on your business.

A good starting point for you may be:

- month vs. the previous month
- month vs. the year-to-date monthly average

- month vs. the same month last year

BUT you still have to come back to the fact that you'd rather web traffic stayed the same and sales went up than web traffic went up and sales went down. Right?

Remember, "hits" stands for "How Idiots Track Sales".

Look at your traffic, but not to the expense of conversion tracking. In an ideal world, you want it to get to the point where you know how much traffic you need to generate an enquiry or sale. If 10 unique website visits produce one sale and you want to make 100 sales a day – well, even we can work that one out! You need to generate 1,000 unique visits a day. So how can you do that and what will it cost?

And keep revisiting your ad targeting. Looking at *who* you're driving to your website. This should be a weekly task. If you know 10 visits give you one sale, what could you do to make 10 visits give you two sales? Without spending more, we mean! Is there dead wood in your targeting that you could strip out? A demographic to remove? Or a new demographic to add and test?

## CONVERSIONS

Bear in mind that conversion tracking might not show the *entire* story, whether that's Google Ad conversions or Facebook Ad conversions.

Let's say your analytics show you that a Facebook Ad campaign is costing you £10 per sale. Now if that £10 cost is generating you £100 in sales, happy days. But if whatever you're selling makes you £2, you may not be happy On paper, it might look like you're £8 worse off, as in you've earned £2 but "lost" £10.

BUT what you need to factor into the equation is all the other clicks your ad campaign has generated, included in that £10 cost. It may have only made you one sale directly, but it has (hopefully) got lots of other targeted people to your website... they just haven't bought yet. And, if you're retargeting like you should be, those people will be encouraged to come back.

So it's a case of looking at the <u>overall</u> picture. Don't get us wrong; the goal is to get the best of both worlds. To make a directly accountable profit on an ad campaign, but to drum up lots of potential new business "for free". If what you're selling makes you £2 but has only cost you 20p to make, AND it's driven other people to your site, well it's Christmas, baby!

## SEO

Ah, the crazy world of Search Engine Optimization.

It's important, yes. You want your website to rank well in the search engines. But would we ever *rely* on it? Nope.

Rely on paid-for ads, especially if you want results <u>now</u>. SEO is a long-haul strategy and – to a certain extent – the goalposts are always being moved, which is out of your hands. When it comes to ads, *you* have more control.

Now, you don't want to be the saddo sat there googling his own business all the time. You may laugh, but lots of business owners do this. Unsuccessful business owners (naturally). The people who don't even realise Google will skew the results based on your previous searches. You have to do an "incognito" search to get virgin results.

You do, however, need some kind of handle on how your website is performing in terms of SEO. How does your website rank for your key search terms?

There are numerous SEO reporting tools. Some are free, some cost a little and others cost more because they offer you advice to improve your SEO, rather than just feeding back.

We got bored of being let down and hopping SEO suppliers, so we partnered with some techies to develop our own. It's software that tells you the good, the bad, the ugly and how to maximize things. You can even tell it how much time you want to dedicate to your SEO per month and it will provide the most time-sensitive solutions. Cool, eh?

With SEO, a lot of businesses focus solely on the big searches and forget about the low hanging fruit. Terms relating to your industry that fewer people will be searching for, but fewer competitors will be fighting over. It's like what we said earlier about posting on socials late at night; fewer eyeballs but fewer businesses posting.

But again, the best way to keep tabs on your SEO is to sign up to an SEO tool.

Do your research, take advantage of any free trials and see what gives. The proof will be in the pudding. Your SEO score will go up, stay the same or *gulp* go down.

Just be aware that if you're in a highly competitive market, you're spending time and money on your SEO and it's not making a blind bit of difference, you may be better off investing that time and money into Google Ads. This is the only guaranteed way to get onto page one of Google. Always.

## SOCIAL MEDIA CONTENT

Earlier, we talked about focusing on reach and engagement when it comes to social media, and cost per click if you're running social media ads – which you should be.

We've banged on about that enough. There are loads of other numbers you could look at, but nine times out of ten, they won't make your boat go any faster.

Where you *would* be wise to invest your test and measure time, is looking at the types of social media content and ads that work best for you.

Hardly anybody does this, so it's a great opportunity.

Is there a type of post that resonates well with your audience? If so, do more of that. Not *only* that but more of it. Too much of a good thing and all.

Facebook makes the testing and measuring of content success easy. Page Insights tell you everything you need to know. You can easily export the information to Excel, where you'll see a whole swathe of numbers available.

But again, *focus on reach and engagement.*

Unless you've got a few video posts – then you should look at how long people watch your videos for. Do they watch for a few seconds and get bored? Or have you posted videos that have held people's attention until at least halfway through? If so, what was it about those videos that worked?

Another thing most people overlook is the type of picture that resonates on social media, and even the type of text.

You know to use non-stock imagery if at all possible. Photos you have taken yourself. Or, if it has to be stock, not the boring stock that all your competitors use. There are only so many pictures of a desk that people can see! You'll never stand out that way. But is there a *kind* of photo that works best for you? Is there a correlation between the imagery in your most successful posts?

If there is, do more of that. Again, not *exclusively*; just more of.

If it's photos of certain members of your team that get higher reach and engagement, hey, go with that. Other members of your team may get precious, so bring it back to the numbers. It's in the best interest of the business to follow the numbers, no matter what they reveal.

You can't risk losing potential sales just because Joe's got the arse that he's not in any of the pics.

When it comes to the kind of text that works best, the main comparison is **long-form vs. short-form**. It's worth testing this on your organic posts *and* ads.

Most of the time, short-form does the job. We're talking about a couple of lines of text, usually short enough to fit above the fold on a mobile. No need to press "read more".

But this isn't always the case. Some of Codebreak's best performing ads have been long-form. A real meaty sell to warm people up enough to click the link. We *always* test short-form and long-form when it comes to ads.

With long-form posts and ads, still keep your sentences and paragraphs short. That rule stays the same. Lots of line breaks with a few emojis chucked in for added visuals.

Please note that <u>things change</u>. People, people's moods, their environment, social media algorithms – so it's never a case of testing and measuring what works best and staying with that forever. Just because images of men gazing into the sunset accompanied by long-form text work the best now, it doesn't mean this will be the case next month. You don't need to check 50 times a week, but fortnightly at least.

With the best-performing images you have, be sure to save them in a suitably labelled shared folder, to come back to time and time again.

With one of our health club clients, we had a photo taken of four of their members grinning to the camera after a group exercise class. The quality was good, but nothing spectacular. It really just captured the high they were on. We have used that same photos dozens of times, in different posts and different ads.

Ultimately, this is all about business growth and balance.

Without getting all Mr Miyagi on you, you want to find out what works best for you, but still keep practising, honing and refining. When you practice, out there on the battlefield, you find out what's changing and you adapt accordingly.

Do what you've always done, and you'll get what you've always gotten.

So many businesses find something that works in their marketing and then stick with that blindly without ongoing testing. They're almost glad it's over. Like in the old days when business owners would bung an ad in *The Yellow Pages* and breathe a sigh of relief. "Thank God for that. That's my marketing done for another year..."

Other businesses get bored quickly and move onto shiny new things, taking their eye off what has actually been working for them.

Again, you need <u>balance</u>.

Go trim that bonsai tree.

**END.**

# ABOUT THE AUTHORS

## ANDY RAO

Andy Rao is a UK business owner, investor and advocate of Marketing That Sells™. After ten years' media employment, working on ad campaigns for the likes of Vodafone and Barclays, Andy set out on his own to help small to medium-sized businesses get results from their marketing. Not just brand awareness but actual sales, which is what puts food on clients' tables.

Having successfully built two advertising companies, Andy partnered with award-winning marketer and graphic designer, Joel Stone, to form the business growth agency, Codebreak.

His wealth of experience makes him highly sought as a direct response copywriter although, as his father said, is officially trained in nothing.... Andy loves helping business owners achieve more money and freedom through better marketing. And, over the years, he has made millions of pounds for hundreds of them. He has just one rule – don't be a dick.

## JOEL STONE

Joel Stone is a marketer and a disciple of business strategy. After seeing the devastation of the recession between 2007 and 2009, he decided to leave employment and set up in business for himself. Having built a successful design agency, he partnered with Andy Rao in 2019 to form the radical marketing agency, Codebreak.

Having previously helped brands including GlaxoSmithKline, Diageo, Beta Tools, and Channel 4, his work has been seen all over the world. He takes pride in applying techniques normally reserved for huge corporations to SMEs throughout the UK and beyond. A Facebook accredited, Shopify partner, case studies of Joel's work have featured in Design Week, The Drum and Social Media Today.

As co-host of the Stay Hungry podcast, Joel regularly interviews marketing experts from all over the world. Having started from scratch, the podcast is now one of the most popular marketing shows in the UK.

In their first book, Andy and Joel pull together the definitive marketing strategy they have learnt through practical application and enthusiasm with accountable results. If you're looking for theory from gurus who prefer standing on stages to standing in trenches, Stay Hungry won't be for you.

# ACKNOWLEDGEMENTS

## ANDY

Emma - My wife, partner in crime, best friend, rock... I could go on. I would say everything I do, I do it for you, but that bloody Bryan Adams got there first.

Maddie and Holly - You complete me and remind me about balance and priorities.

Mum - Hopefully dad would be proud. You made me who I am. So it's all your fault! Those teenage years were a dream, eh...?!

Joel - I never thought I'd meet someone as tenacious and stubborn as me. And that's a good thing.... Stronger in business together.

Charlie – You reminded me that amongst all the new-fangled tech, "old school" marketing principles and psychology will always prevail.

## JOEL

Hannah – The most positive, forward-looking and refreshing person I have ever met. You patch me together when I'm breaking myself apart, you hold me up when others wouldn't, and best of all, you're my wife.

Mum – Nobody will fully understand what you put yourself through to ensure Callum and I made it to adulthood. I've never seen love and determination like yours in anyone else. Your tenacity to protect those close to you is unreal.

Callum – Intelligent, kind, sensitive, and gifted. You make me laugh when I'm at my worst and humble me when I'm at my best. The best brother anyone could wish for.

Andy – You've taught me more in ten years than I knew it was possible to learn. We're just scratching the surface.

Charlie - You push me beyond where I hoped I could go, and you keep pushing! You've nudged me along to discover my best self and encouraged me to better it.

# STAY HUNGRY

**MARKETING PODCAST**

**Staying hungry is the key to success. Listen in on this podcast for tips and anecdotes from Joel, Andy, and guests as they discuss marketing strategies, techniques, business mindset, successes and failures, and demonstrate to you just what it takes to market a growing business.**

Ready for more? Stay Hungry is available on all major podcast platforms. Visit codebreak.co.uk/podcast to listen.

# NOTES

# NOTES

# NOTES

# NOTES

# NOTES

# NOTES

# NOTES

# NOTES

Printed in Great Britain
by Amazon

76501686R00087